# Developing Resilient Youth

*Classroom Activities for*
*Social-Emotional Competence*

**William G. Nicoll, PhD**

abbott press®
A DIVISION OF WRITER'S DIGEST

**Developing Resilient Youth**
**Classroom Activities for Social-Emotional Competence**

*Abbott Press books may be ordered through booksellers or by contacting:*

*Abbott Press*
*1663 Liberty Drive*
*Bloomington, IN 47403*
*www.abbottpress.com*
*Phone: 1-866-697-5310*

*Because of the dynamic nature of the Internet, any web addresses or links contained in this book may have changed since publication and may no longer be valid. The views expressed in this work are solely those of the author and do not necessarily reflect the views of the publisher, and the publisher hereby disclaims any responsibility for them.*

*Any people depicted in stock imagery provided by Thinkstock are models, and such images are being used for illustrative purposes only.*

*Certain stock imagery © Thinkstock.*

*ISBN: 978-1-4582-0078-5 (sc)*
*ISBN: 978-1-4582-0079-2 (e)*

*Library of Congress Control Number: 2011917690*

*Printed in the United States of America*

*Abbott Press rev. date:  10/20/2011*

# Contents

# Foreward

How do we begin to transform and re-direct our schools from their increasingly narrow focus on the 3 R's of 'Reading, 'Riting and 'Rithmetic and high stakes testing to a broader recognition that there is much more involved in preparing our youth for successful lives? National Polls continually reveal that people are deeply concerned about the quality of our schools and want significant changes in our current educational practices. Doubts are expressed as to the effectiveness of our schools in preparing children to be successful in the new, global economy. Such doubts and the subsequent calls for improving schools are nothing new. Concerns about our educational systems have been continuously expressed for the better part of the past century. In the United States alone, we have witnessed numerous national reports critical of our schools and endless calls for educational reform. For example, in the early half of the century there was the Progressive Movement of John Dewey. This movement was echoed abroad with the education reform initiatives of individuals such as Maria Montessori and Alfred Adler. In the 1950's, there was the Conant Report and the NDEA Act to reform and improve our public education system. In the 1980's, we had the "A Nation At Risk" report followed by reforms efforts such as "Blueprint 2000" and "No Child Left Behind". Unfortunately, none of these efforts have proven very successful.

The reason for these continuing failures to improve the quality of education, and subsequently the readiness of our youth to become responsible, competent and productive members of society, may well lie in H.L. Mencken's famous quote that, *"For every complex problem, there is a clear and straightforward solution; that is wrong!"*. Indeed, one dimensional, and politically motivated reform attempts are doomed to fail. While we've witnessed unparalleled changes socially, politically and economically yet our public education systems have continued to cling to the same paradigms, strategies and methods of prior decades and indeed, centuries. The problem is complex. Complex problems require complex, systemic solutions.

Calls for educational reform are heard in many countries around the world. A common theme increasingly heard among these calls is echoed in the words of Vaclav Havel, former President of the Czech Republic, when he stated, *". . . the most important thing is a new concept of education. At all levels, schools must cultivate a spirit of free and independent thinking in the students . . . schools will have to be humanized . . . schools must lead young people to become self-confident, participating citizens"*. While traditional, basic academic skills are still vital, over 66% of the U.S. population now recognize that a much broader range of social-emotional skills are also needed and should be incorporated into the school curriculum (21st Century Skills, 2001). Numerous studies have confirmed this need for a broader approach to improving the education and preparation of our youth.

The Developing Resilient Youth (DRY) program is based on the premise that Resilience is the missing fourth 'R' in education. Resilience is suggested here as being the key to transforming our schools into more effective educational institutions. Fostering resilience in youth involves both the teaching of essential social-emotional competencies, and the creation of more supportive, empowering school, classroom and family environments. The DRY program is thus offered as being but one component (i.e., the teaching of essential social-emotional skills) in a much larger, more complex and systemic strategy for transforming our schools and developing capable, resilient youth.

The goal of the Developing Resilient Youth program is to provide all students with those essential social-emotional skills identified by the resilience research as necessary for successfully fulfilling the full complement of adult roles. By implementing the program, schools effectively reintroduce the lost "Fourth R" in education. Students are more effectively prepared to become cooperative, responsible, competent, productive and contributing citizens in an increasingly global society. Implementing the Developing Resilient Youth program will contribute to the creation of a more positive school culture, foster more positive classroom climates, improve student learning motivation, improve academic achievement, reduce bullying and social aggression, and foster improved home-school collaboration in the raising of resilient, capable youth.

# Introduction

# Building the Transformative School
### A resilience-based paradigm

Calls for new, innovative classroom practices and educational reforms have been relatively constant over the past century. However, as Kliebard (1990) noted in his review of educational reform efforts, "little has changed". Indeed, many educators have grown increasingly cynical and pessimistic about any educational reform ideas or new instructional methods purported to be cutting edge, innovative educational practice. As far back as 1922, W.W. Charters referred to the history of education as ". . . *a chronicle of fads*". Other dismissive terms such as "fads and foibles", "frills", or "pendulum swings" have continued to be commonplace characterizations of new practices set forth as being innovative and certain to substantially improve school and classroom effectiveness. Despite the "innovative new practices", the reform movements, and the legislatively mandated accountability programs, education's search for its own version of the elusive "philosopher's stone", that one strategy that will instantly turn all students into high achieving, college bound graduates, has continuously proven to be unsuccessful. Indeed, it has been no more successful than the original search by the alchemist's of the middle-ages seeking their mythical philosopher's stone that would turn transform any element into gold.

Why is it then that the more things change, the more they stay the same in our schools? Perhaps it is due to our failure to differentiate between innovative and transformative change. Transformative change involves the adopting of a fundamentally new perspective to a problem, in other words a paradigm shift. Such paradigm shifts lead to qualitatively different solutions that move us to higher levels of functioning (King, 2005; Mezirow, 2000). Transformative Change in education requires just such a Copernican Shift to our dominant paradigm. We need to rethink our understanding of the educational process and rethink the tacit assumptions about effective schools and the purpose of education; these tacit assumptions guide our daily perceptions, decisions and instructional practices. Systems theory refers to transformative change as, Second Order change; a metamorphosis, or fundamental change, in form or character. As Einstein put it so simply, *"You can't solve a problem with the same thinking that created it."*

Unfortunately, most new educational methods and reform efforts have embraced only innovative change. Innovation, by definition, involves initiating something new, a different method or, to alter something that is already established. Systems theory refers to such innovative change as First Order change; that is, new ways of doing the same old thing. While new, innovative instructional techniques and school organization strategies are constantly put forward, they remain fundamentally consistent with the dominant paradigm guiding education practice. Even though leading researchers on effective schools have repeatedly noted that instructional, curricular variables appear to play a neutral role in school effectiveness, still most schools continue to focus almost exclusively on this single area for staff development and innovative school improvement. Transformative change requires Second Order change processes; this involves a fundamental change in our guiding paradigms and basic assumptions.

Initiating transformative thinking and transformative change is never easy. Both people and institutions have a natural tendency to resist real change and maintain the status quo, the familiar. Thus, schools will tend to embrace innovation but resist transformation. As noted by one of the foremost Transformative Leaders of our time, Dee W. Hock, Founder and CEO of VISA, "*The problem is never how to get new, innovative thoughts into your mind, but how to get old one's out. Every mind is a building with archaic furniture, clean out a corner of your mind and creativity will instantly fill it.*"

Through the adoption of a fundamentally new perspective, an alternative paradigm, educators can truly transform our schools and improve their ability to produce academically capable and socially competent, responsible youth. Adopting such a transformative perspective enables us to view our schools through "new eyes" and empowers educators to transcend traditional school practices and move their 'good schools' toward becoming 'great schools', their struggling students toward becoming successful students, and all students to becoming more productive, responsible and contributing citizens in a global society.

Consistent with Dee Hock's statement on transformative change, the developing of transformative classrooms and transformative schools requires that we clean out our archaic furniture; those long held, unquestioned, tacit assumptions about education, teaching, student learning, and school organization. In the age of high stakes testing, many school systems have come to measure success merely by the achievement scores on state or national tests. The model suggested by the Developing Resilient Youth program is to go beyond mere academic achievement and address the larger issue of, what type of people (citizens, employees, leaders, etc) are we preparing in our schools? It is our collective mindset and underlying assumptions as to what constitutes an effective school and a quality education that requires transformative change.

### *Resilience as the Copernican Shift*

The resilience research of the past two decades provides a framework for just such transformative change in our schools. And what would such a truly transformative approach to improving our schools school look like if based in the resilience research? How might this paradigm be translated into practical school programs and practices? The "Little Red Schoolhouse" pictured on page 7 provides a visual representation of the resilience-based, Transformative School. As with any construction project, building a transformative school structure would begin by first laying a solid foundation. The foundation of the resilience-based, transformative school is reflected in its shared philosophy, vision and mission. This might be something to the effect of, "***All children are Welcome and Every child***

***will Succeed*!**" This creates an inclusive, inviting school climate in which the labeling of children and segregating of students according to assumed abilities and potential versus disabilities, disorders or dysfunctions is rejected. Once such a foundation is laid as the base of our transformative schoolhouse, building of the new, resilience-based school requires then putting up the support walls that are strong and viable.

The first support wall consists of creating supportive social environments in the school and home. The resilience-based school would seek to train all teachers, school leaders and parents in effective parenting and positive classroom management strategies. Research has demonstrated that the authoritative/democratic style of parental and classroom leadership leads to improved outcomes both academically and socially. The authoritative parenting style has been consistently linked with higher academic achievement, better student relationships with peers and adult/authority figures, higher aspirations, and more positive social behavior. Research on the characteristics of highly effective teachers has similarly identified their teacher-student relationship style as being consistent with the authoritative leadership approach. Indeed research points to the three factors of high caring, high expectations, and growth mindsets in which a teacher believes in every student's ability to succeed, as the key ingredients for positive classroom climates and optimally effective teaching.

The second support wall of our resilience-based, transformative school structure would consist of integrating social-emotional learning into the overall school curriculum and culture. The resilience-based, transformative school would seek to develop student's social-emotional competence as an integral component within the school's overall curricular organization and not as merely a stand alone "classroom guidance" or "character education" add-on initiative. The Developing Resilient Youth program identifies five basic social-emotional competencies (skills) from the resilience research as providing the second support wall: Understanding & Respecting Self and Others, Empathy, Positive/Constructive Communication, Cooperation, and Responsible Contribution. These five social-emotional competencies are actively taught, modeled and fostered throughout the school curriculum. Schools that actively teach social-emotional competencies find that academic achievement increases by up to 17% while problem behaviors, bullying, and social aggression dramatically decrease (Zins, et.al, 2004).

The roof on our resilience-based, transformative school consists of assisting students in identifying and exploring their goals and aspirations in life. This includes not only the traditional focus on career and academic goals but thinking as well about their future home/family life, their social and community responsibilities, health and recreation interests, and the spiritual/ethical principles that will guide their lives as world citizens.

Finally, with a solid school structure consisting of a solid philosophical foundation, strong supporting walls and a roof now in place, we are ready to bring in the interior design specialists with the school's furnishings. The "furniture", in our transformative schoolhouse consists of the academic curriculum, teaching methods and the strategies of effective instruction. The current, dominant educational paradigm driving our schools is focused almost exclusively on re-arranging the furniture in our schools; what might be termed, "innovations in educational interior design". Unfortunately, this leaves the foundation and structural strength of our schools largely ignored. A resiliency-based, transformative school would take a much wider, more inclusive perspective and consider the total spectrum of research as to factors most important in developing capable, productive and responsible youth. The transformative school would focus on improving the quality of the supportive school structures. Parents, teachers and school administrators would work collaboratively to actively assess and strengthen the quality and supportiveness of the overall school social environment in addition to the quality of the curricular "furniture".

# Developing a Transformative School:

## A Resiliency Based Paradigm

**Life Goals:**
Family/Home, Education/Career
Community/Social, Recreation/Health
Spiritual/Ethical

**Support Wall #1:**
**Supportive Environments**

Authoritative Parenting &
Teaching Styles

High Caring/High Expectations

Opportunities for experiencing
4 Goals of Positive Behavior

High Involvement/Support

**Academic Competencies:**

**Reading / Language Arts**

**Mathematics**

**Science / Technology**

**Arts & Humanities**

**Social Sciences**

**Health & Recreation**

**Languages**

**Support Wall #2:**
**Social-Emotional
Competencies**

Understanding &
Respecting Self/Others

Empathy Skills

Communication Skills

Cooperation Skills

Responsible Contribution
Skills

**Foundational School Philosophy:**

*ALL Children are Welcome and Every child will Succeed!*

# Chapter 1

# Developing Resilient Youth:
# A research based rationale

The intended function of our public educational system has been, since its inception, the development of responsible, capable and productive youth fully prepared to assume their full complement of social, occupational and familial roles in society. Success in life requires both academic competence and social-emotional competence: i.e. the ability to "work and play well with others". Unfortunately, education has, over the past decades, increasingly tended to focus almost exclusively on developing students' academic competence and largely abandoned the task of developing social-emotional competence. This failure to develop both skill sets – academic and social-emotional - has resulted in not only deficiencies in student's readiness for the workplace and college but increased social adjustment problems as well. Inadequately developed social-emotional competence limits or negates the effectiveness of instructional based attempts to improve academic achievement. The Developing Resilient Youth program seeks to provide a model for transforming our schools by integrating the resilience research emphasis on supportive environments and social-emotional competencies with academic instruction methods. Further, the Developing Resilient Youth program contributes to transforming school practice by integrating social-emotional learning, academic instruction, and home-school collaboration.

Historically, character education or social-emotional education has been a priority in our educational system. In founding Exeter Academy and Philips Exeter Academy, Dr. John Phillips envisioned public education in the United States as involving the development of young people's academic ability, intellectual curiosity and tenacity, and human decency and good character. In 1781, Phillips stated the mission of his school was that, *"Above all it is expected that the attention of the instructors to the disposition of the minds and morals of the youth under their charge will exceed every other care; well considering that though goodness without knowledge is weak and feeble, yet knowledge without goodness is dangerous, and that both united form the noblest character and lay the sweet foundation of usefulness to mankind"*. The sociologist, Ashley Montague would later echo these words saying, *". . . first and foremost and always in the order of importance as a principle reason for the existence of the school . . . we must train for humanity . . . for all the knowledge in the world is worse than useless if it is not humanely understood and humanely used. An intelligence that is not humane is the most dangerous thing in the world"*.

This point is illustrated below by an alumni list from two hypothetical schools (fig. 2). School 'A' can boast of an alumni "Hall of Fame" that consists of academically high performing former students. Unfortunately, the list consists of some rather infamous individuals who used their intelligence and education in a manner that proved quite harmful to many people around the world. School 'B', on the

1

William G. Nicoll, PhD

other hand, consists of an alumni "Hall of Fame" comprised of individuals who were all academically low performing students but who possessed social-emotional competence. Their resilience would later serve to motivate them on to higher intellectual accomplishments and consequently, to making substantial positive contributions to the lives of people all over the world. How then do we determine which is the "effective school"? Utilizing the current reform paradigm with its primary criteria of academic performance, only School 'A' can be clearly declared a "School of Excellence". However, most of us would probably much prefer a school that produced students more like that of School 'B'; students who will make a positive, responsible contributions to our society.

---

## Which is the more Effective School?

### Alumni Hall of Fame

| SCHOOL 'A' | | SCHOOL 'B' | |
|---|---|---|---|
| Ivan Boesky | Investment Broker | Isaac Newton | Scientist |
| Bernard Ebbers | (WorldCom CEO) | Thomas Alva Edison | Inventor |
| Dennis Kozlowski | (Tyco CEO) | Albert Einstein | Mathematician |
| Saloth Sar | (aka: Pol Pot, Cambodia) | Giacomo Puccini | Composer |
| Slobodan Milosevic | (Yugoslavia & Serbia) | James Watt | Inventor |
| Richard Sorosky | (HealthSouth CEO) | Henry Ford | Inventor |
| Ken Lay | (Enron CEO) | Pablo Picasso | Artist |
| Jeff Skilling | (Enron CEO) | G. K. Chesterton | Author/Editor |
| Ivar Kreuger | (the Match King - Sweden) | Winston Churchill | Statesman |
| Charles Keating | (Lincoln Savings & Loan) | Charles Darwin | Naturalist |
| Fidel Castro | (Cuba) | Luciano Pavarotti | Tenor |
| Bernie Madoff | (Invesment Broker) | Alfred Adler | Psychiatrist |
| Joseph Stalin | (Russia) | John Lennon | Composer |
| Charles Taylor | (Liberia) | Steven Spielberg | Movie Director |
| Kim Il Sung | (Korea 1948- 94) | Orville Wright | Inventor |
| Leopold II | (Belgian Congo) | Jerry Lewis | Comedian |
| Augusto Pinochet | (Chile) | John Cheever | Writer/ Pulitzer |
| Than Shwe | (Myanmar) | Dr. Abdul Kalam | President India |

[Figure 2]

---

Interestingly, despite the well documented importance of social-emotional competencies, teacher education training programs in North America are not required, and typically do not, include coursework on social-emotional learning. Rather, the focus is on the teaching of only those academic skills deemed essential for "academic excellence". Indeed, many would argue that the focus of education has, of late, grown ever more narrow until it now focuses almost exclusively on those skills measured by high stakes testing.

Education has remained rather ambivalent as to what extent the schools should address the challenge of developing students' social-emotional competencies and character. While the past century has witnessed periodic movements calling for character education and classroom guidance programs to address students' social, moral or character development, the result has typically been short lived and more likely to embody ideologically or politically based agendas rather than research based programs.

What accounts for this ambivalence among educators regarding integrating social-emotional learning along with academic learning? By continuing to view the function of schools as solely that of instilling academic skills in children, educators ignore attempts to consider anything that might distract from this solitary goal. A transformative change in how we understand the preparation of children and adolescents for productive, successful lives involves a return to Dr. Phillips' initial idea that both academic and social-emotional competencies are necessary for a true education; indeed, either without the other weakens our society.

The Resilience paradigm alters and broadens our focus. We move from asking the old questions of, *"What is wrong with this student; What instructional method is needed?; or "What neurological disorder, deficit or dysfunction impedes this student from learning and/or causes such behavioral problems?."* Instead, we begin to ask the more useful question of, *"What factors are conducive to healthy student development, higher achievement, and lead youth to handle problems, overcome obstacles and develop into responsible, cooperative, productive, useful, well-adjusted and contributing members of our global society?"* The resiliency research points to two primary, inter-related factors as leading to such positive academic and social adjustment outcomes in youth:

1. The development of a set of essential social-emotional competencies and,
2. The presence of positive, supportive social environments in the home, school and community (Benard, 1991; 2004).

Developing Resilient Youth (DRY) assists educators in designing and implementing a comprehensive program to improve student social-emotional competencies while also improving home-school collaboration as well as both the classroom and school climate. By so doing, both improved social-emotional adjustment and improved academic achievement are realized; these two factors are but two sides of the same coin. Thus, a synergic effect occurs when both skill sets are improved! As the Viennese Psychiatrist, Alfred Adler (1929) stated while advocating for educational reform in the first quarter of the last century, *"the teacher who takes the time to work on students' social development will find [his or her] job simultaneously amplified and simplified. It is unquestionably far simpler and more efficient to teach the well adjusted, cooperative and responsible child than it is to nag, prod and threaten along the maladjusted, uncooperative, irresponsible child"*. Research evidence indicates that when such a program is implemented, schools will realize not only improvements in academic achievement but improvement in classroom and school climate, home-school partnerships and overall student behavior. In addition, with the improvement of student social-emotional competencies and the development of more supportive social environments (classroom, school and home), student resilience is developed. This, in turn, research indicates, leads to decreases in: the drop-out and truancy rates, incidents of bullying and social aggression, delinquency, substance abuse, and other behavioral adjustment problems among our youth.

**Research Evidence for the Teaching of Social-Emotional Competence**

Research evidence has now clearly identified social-emotional competence as being at least as important as academic skills in determining future life success; perhaps even more important. Johnson & Johnson (1989) concluded in their research review that social skills appear to be the most important set of skills influencing one's future employability, productiveness and career success. The 2008 College and Workplace Readiness Report supported the same observations. Comparing those competencies which researchers across three fields have identified as critical to college and workplace success (i.e., healthy youth development, college readiness and workplace readiness), the report concluded that in addition to academic skills a variety of psychological and social skills are also vital to success in the transition to adulthood. Unfortunately, many, if not most, of these skills are not included in the school's curriculum. Particularly absent, the report noted, are social-emotional competencies such as: problem solving/critical thinking, self-management/self-understanding, personal and social responsibility, ethical/moral character as well as skills in cooperation, understanding self & others (including other cultures), communication and conflict resolution/tolerance.

The National Research Council and the Institute of Medicine (Eccles & Gootman, 2002) concluded that supportive relationships appear to serve as "critical mediums" of development providing the opportunity for the healthy physical, intellectual, psychological and social growth of youth. Research has also identified the authoritative/democratic style of parent, teacher and school administrator leadership as being highly correlated with positive outcomes in youth. The authoritative/democratic parenting and teaching leadership style focuses on the three factors of warmth/connection, guidance/regulation and psychological autonomy/responsibility. Such parenting and classroom leadership styles have been found to result in higher academic achievement, greater psychological adjustment, social competence, self-reliance, creativity and responsibility (Barber & Olsen, 1997; Cohen & Rice, 1997; Dornbusch, et. al, 1987; Lahey, et.al, 1999; Paulsen, et.al, 1997). The national longitudinal study on adolescent health found a sense of belonging or connectedness with one's family and one's school to be the two most powerful predictors of positive youth adjustment (Resnick, et. al., 1997). Numerous studies have identified supportive and caring relationships within schools to promote higher academic achievement, higher academic motivation and more positive social adjustment (McNeely & Falci, 2004; Libbey, 2004).

Developmental psychologists now widely recognize social-emotional competence, or resilience, as a significant indicator of children's overall positive adaptation or wellness. The social-emotional competencies identified by the resilience research have been found to be at least as important as academic skills for determining future life success, and perhaps even more important (Benard, 2004; Goleman, 1995, 2006). Social-emotional competencies such as responsiveness to others, empathy, caring, communication skills, humor, positive relationship skills, flexibility and adaptability in solving social problems are the key attributes of successful youth. When these social competencies are present, youth are more likely to develop into healthy, competent young adults even when there is the presence of adverse (at-risk) life situations (Benard, 1991; Dweck, 2000; 2006).

Conversely, most of the adjustment problems manifested by children and adolescents have been directly linked to inadequate social skills or social competencies. Inadequate social competence has also been empirically demonstrated to be predictive of adult psychiatric problems. Research evidence has established a direct link between most of the problems currently manifested among our youth such as, substance abuse, violence, crime, depression, school failure and inadequately developed social competencies

Research on resilient children (i.e., at-risk youth who seem immune to the negative consequences normally associated with their life circumstances) indicates that social competencies such as responsiveness to others, empathy, caring, communication skills, humor, positive social relationships, flexibility and adaptability in solving social problems are key attributes explaining their development into healthy, competent young adults (Bernard, 1991). Goleman (1995) and Mayer & Salovey (1997) have termed this social competence, Emotional Intelligence (EQ), which they define as involving the knowing of one's own feelings, making good decisions in life, being motivated, remaining optimistic, having empathy toward others and being able to get along with, to work cooperatively with, and to lead others.

Fortunately, recent studies have also indicated that a child's long-term social and emotional adaptation, academic and cognitive development and citizenship skills can, indeed, be enhanced through exposure to opportunities for developing and strengthening social-emotional competence during childhood (Diekstra, 2008; Payton, et. al., 2008; Zins, et. al., 2004). Goleman, in reviewing the related research, notes that EQ appears to serve as a meta-ability determining how well one uses all of his or her intellectual and academic skills (Goleman, 1995). He goes on to note that research evidence indicates that Emotional Intelligence appears to be a better determinant of future life success (career, familial and social) than academic performance or general intelligence. Echoing the words of Alfred Adler some 70 years earlier, Goleman (1995) suggested that the educational system should take a more active role in developing students' social-emotional intelligence (i.e., social competence) and by so doing would better prepare students for both academic success and the assumption of a useful, contributive place in the larger global society.

Given the significant body of empirical evidence linking social-emotional competence to both academic success and future life success as well as the inverse correlation with numerous adjustment problems of youth, it would only seem appropriate for educators to redirect their efforts increasingly toward the implementation of a broader, developmental approach to educating our youth. Such a developmental paradigm would include the development of resilience in youth (i.e. mental health or positive social adjustment). As the California Task Force to Promote Self-Esteem and Personal and Social Responsibility (1990) so aptly put it, we need to work toward the development of a "Social Vaccine" for youth. We need to develop programs and practices in our schools and communities that create positive child-rearing environments and promote the development of key social competencies so as to immunize youth from the myriad of social stressors and problems they will encounter over the course of their lives. This is the goal of the Developing Resilient Youth program!

**Bullying & Social Aggression**

The issue of bullying, or social aggression, has become an increasing concern among educators and parents over these past few decades. The prevalence rate varies amongst the numerous studies. However, all the research studies indicate a pronounced problem as student reports of being involved in bullying, the victim of bullying, or aware of bullying in their school range from 29 to 86 percent. Studies also clearly indicate that teachers and administrators greatly underestimate the frequency of bullying behavior in their schools. The "*but, we're a good school, that just doesn't happen here*" myth contributes to many teachers and school administrators developing a perceptual "blind spot" toward bullying. Ironically, the research indicates that bullying behaviors actually increase in schools with a record of high achievement in academics, athletics and extra-curricular programs. A dominant school culture that emphasizes being "better than" can inadvertently foster and condone a one-upmanship, superiority, and competitive climate that creates fertile soil in which bullying and social aggression may grow and develop.

The negative impact of bullying on students just cannot be denied. It is reflected in numerous television and newspaper documentations of various acts of school violence, hazing, harassment and assaults of a physical, sexual, psychological and emotional nature. Left unrecognized and unaddressed, such acts of bullying have even escalated to incidents of teen suicide and retaliatory acts of violence including school shootings. A report in 2002 by the U.S. Secret Service and Department of Education concluded that bullying played a significant role in many school shootings. In a majority of the incidents, the attackers felt bullied, persecuted, or injured by others prior to the attack.

By creating an unsafe environment and a sense of "disconnectedness" for both targeted victims and students fearing victimization, bullying also can contribute to lowered academic achievement, increased truancy and early school withdrawal (Juvonen & Wentzel, 1996, McDougall, Hymel, Olweus, 1991, 1992; Vaillancourt & Mercer, 2001, Parker & Asher, 1987). The National Longitudinal Study on Adolescent Health found school connectedness to be associated with higher academic achievement and inversely correlated with adolescent violence, substance abuse, early sexual activity, and drop-outs (Resnick, et al, 1997). However, bullying tactics such as social isolation, intimidation, humiliation or rejection work against school connectedness and can often lead to serious academic and social-behavioral adjustment problems. Overt, covert and cyber bullying strategies all involve abusive interpersonal interactions leading victims to either internalize their problems (e.g., low self-esteem, depression and anxiety) or to externalize their problems (e.g., anti-social behavior, conduct disorders, delinquency).

At the same time, research has indicated that common school responses such as anti-bullying campaigns, zero tolerance policies, and attempts to identify and punish or expel bullies are largely ineffective. However, the implementing of more comprehensive programs designed to improve the supportive quality of the school culture and create supportive classroom climates while developing positive social-emotional competencies in youth does appear to be an effective, long-term approach to decreasing bullying behavior in schools (Twemlow, et. al 2001; Twemlow & Sacco, 2008).

Bullying occurs in many different settings. It occurs in families in the form of physical, sexual or psychological/emotional and verbal abuse. Also, much as we may dislike admitting it, bullying occurs in some of our schools and classrooms. There are, unfortunately, some teachers, coaches, administrators and staff who have been known to be verbally and psychologically abusive to students. They often resort to bullying tactics such as humiliation, threats, isolation and social rejection under the guise of "school discipline" or classroom behavior management strategies. And in the workplace, supervisors, employers and even colleagues may systematically engage in bullying behaviors toward their targeted victims. This is now referred in the research literature as "workplace bullying" or "mobbing". Unfortunately, no social environment appears to be immune from bullying behaviors.

What then have we learned about bullies and bullying behavior in schools? One of the most important findings is that individuals who engage in acts of bullying tend to be deficient in certain social-emotional skill areas. First of all, they are often lacking in the ability to understand and respect those who are different from themselves. This leads to dehumanizing and stereotyping others as, "those types" who "deserve it" or "don't belong here" or "aren't wanted here". Thus the bully feels entitled to make the different student a target. As Oliner and Oliner note in their book, The Altruistic Personality: Rescuers of Jews in Nazi Europe (1988), anti-Semitism and the maltreatment of Jews was more easily fostered and silently condoned in countries where the Jews and the majority populations tended to live somewhat separately from one another. But, in countries such as Denmark and Italy where the populations were more intermingled and thus known on a personal level among one another, people were far more likely to step forward and hide or protect the Jewish population.

Secondly, bullies are found to be lacking in empathy, the ability to connect with the feelings and perspectives of others. In addition, their communication style, both verbal and non-verbal, is typically negative and destructive with frequent put-downs, insults and demeaning or rejecting statements and actions. Cooperation skills are often found to be lacking among bullies as well. They strive to always appear superior, dominant or in control of situations and others, perhaps out of fear that the only other alternative is to be the dominated, controlled and in the inferior position socially. Finally, bullies avoid taking responsibility for their own actions. The typical response of a bully when confronted about their actions is to use the standard "DMV" response pattern of all abusers: Denial, Minimization, and Victim Blaming. The Developing Resilient Youth program specifically targets the development of these five essential social-emotional competencies. Through the implementation of this program both bullies/abusers themselves and, even more importantly, their classmates develop these five essential social-emotional competencies, a bullying antidote.

Another important thing we've learned about bullying is that bullies can only do what the bystanders allow. The Developing Resilient Youth program helps promote a peer and faculty culture in the school that rejects bullying behaviors and fosters a greater sense of understanding, respect, empathy, inclusion and social responsibility among all students and staff. Bullying behaviors are antithetical to such a classroom climate and school culture. Bullying behavior fails to take root and thrive in such non-fertile terrain. In essence, the Developing Resilient Youth program offers both an antidote to bullying behaviors and a vaccine inoculating children and classrooms from the negative effects of bullying. In the book, The Altruistic Personality, the authors describe how, in 1943, the Danish population, upon hearing that the Nazis were going to round up the Danish Jews and place them into concentration camps, spontaneously organized a plan to ferry all Denmark's Jewish population out of the country, over 7000 of an estimated 7500 in all were evacuated to neutral Sweden. One of the Danish rescuers later explained this heroic act by Denmark's responsible bystanders stating that, "*The basic morality in this little homogeneous country is such that we have been told for generations to be nice to your neighbor, be polite and treat people well. You didn't want anything to happen to your neighbors or friends – so you fought for them . . . People would stop others from doing illegal things; even during blackouts, there was no theft. When the Jewish people came back to Denmark, they found all their property intact, nothing was missing . . . their neighbors and friends took care of it.*" Such is the nature of the school culture which the Developing Resilient Youth strives to foster in all our schools.

**A Developmental Model for Resilience (i.e. mentally healthy individuals)**

Exactly what constitutes a mentally healthy, well adjusted individual has, rather ironically, been insufficiently addressed within the greater mental health field. However, those who have addressed the issue have arrived at very similar conclusions. Abraham Maslow (1964) used the term, social synergy, to indicate that the mentally healthy individual fuses what is good for his/herself with the needs and interests of others. The Viennese psychiatrist, Alfred Adler, suggested the term, gemeinschaftsgefuhl (i.e., community-ship feeling or Social Interest), as the criterion for mental health. This involves an interest in the interests of humankind, a sense of security and feeling at home on this earth through feeling oneself to be connected to others on an equal and cooperative basis (Ansbacher, 1968). The mentally healthy individual, Adler suggested, is able to understand and appreciate the subjective experiences and opinions of others and behaves in a responsible, cooperative and contributive manner in his/her relationships with others. Most of the problems manifested by children and youth, he further noted, could be traced back to insufficient development of this attitude; such youth had received insufficient training in the essential social skills for living in harmony and equality with others; their positive social adjustment had been insufficiently fostered and developed in their primary social environments of family, school and community.

Adler's theory on the development of mentally healthy and socially well-adjusted individuals is quite compatible with the more recent resilience research. His work suggested a developmental stage process for the healthy social emotional development of youth. The developmental stage model adapted from Adler and the more recent resilience research is illustrated in the following figure.

---

## DEVELOPMENTAL STAGES
## *of RESILIENCE*

————————————

**STAGE 1:**     An *INNATE APTITUDE* with the potential for
                development through training

**STAGE 2:**     A set of *OBJECTIVE SOCIAL SKILLS* learned
                Through training in the home, school and community
                - ➤ **Understanding & Respecting Self & Others**
                - ➤ **Empathy**
                - ➤ **Communication**
                - ➤ **Cooperation**
                - ➤ **Responsible Contribution**

**STAGE 3:**     A *SUBJECTIVE ATTITUDE* toward life and others upon which
                we attach meaning to events and make behavioral choices.

(Figure 3)

---

In the first of these developmental stages, resilience (mental health) is viewed as an innate aptitude for cooperative, responsible social living with which we are all born. However, this aptitude for resilience must be further developed through training in the home, school and community. Thus, in the second stage, the child is directly taught those objective social-emotional skills, or competencies, associated with resilience. Five essential social-emotional competencies appear to form the foundation for resilience and positive social-emotional adjustment. These consist of the skills of: a) understanding and respecting oneself and others, b) empathy, c) positive/constructive communication, d) cooperation and, e) responsible contribution.

As the child develops these essential social-emotional competencies, a subjective attitude begins to emerge. In the third and final developmental stage, one comes to value these social-emotional competencies and consequently evaluates his or her actions based upon the degree to which they reflect the five objective social-emotional competencies. As noted by Ryan (1986) regarding moral education, this approach essentially operationalizes Aristotle's idea that one becomes virtuous by performing virtuous acts; kind by doing kind acts; brave by doing brave acts. In the Developing

Resilient Youth program, students develop resilience, i.e., positive psychosocial adjustment, by first learning and practicing the essential social-emotional competency skills. Through the learning of these essential competencies, the development of positive psychosocial adjustment and readiness to act in a socially responsible, empathic, cooperative and contributive manner with others at school, in the workplace, in the family and in the community is fostered.

The Developing Resilient Youth program is consistent with other theories such as the Positive Psychology of Seligman and the concept of Emotional Intelligence (EQ) put forward by Goleman (1995) and Mayer & Salovey (1997). Goleman, for example, defines Emotional Intelligence as involving several dimensions including: knowing one's own feelings, making good decisions in life, being motivated, remaining hopeful and optimistic during setbacks, empathy toward others, getting along with others and, being able to both work with and lead others (O'Neil, 1996). Over the past two decades, a growing body of research evidence has accumulated in support of these ideas. Children who fail to achieve adequate social-emotional competence have a higher probability of being at-risk through adolescence and into adulthood (Ladd, 2000; Parker & Asher, 1987). They are more likely to experience a variety of problems including poor mental health, dropping out of school, low achievement and other school difficulties (Katz & McClellan, 1997).

Without doubt, the research findings argue strongly for the development and implementation of sound, research based developmental guidance programs within our schools. Such programs would seek to foster the development of essential social-emotional competencies while simultaneously creating more positive and supportive school and home environments. Social competence and academic competence are not competing curricular topics in education. Rather, they are necessary if our youth are to be successfully prepared to assume the full complement of adult roles as responsible, cooperative, compassionate and contributive citizens.

# Chapter 2

# Implementing the Developing Resilient Youth Program

The development of students' social-emotional competencies is best accomplished when integrated with the development of students' academic competence. By so doing, teachers can better fulfill the school's role and function in society of preparing youth to lead successful occupational, social and family lives. The Developing Resilient Youth (DRY) classroom guidance program is specifically designed to teach the essential social-emotional competencies most associated with resilience and healthy psychosocial adjustment. Thus, the program empowers youth and provides a much needed *"Social Vaccine"* to immunize our youth from the myriad of social ills in today's society including those of substance abuse, bullying, delinquency, truancy and drop outs, and school failure. At the same time, the program can serve as an *"Antidote"* for these same social and behavioral problems when they have already started to emerge among students.

By integrating instruction in social-emotional competencies with the established academic curriculum, teachers will observe a significant improvement in student interest, learning motivation, depth of understanding, and critical thinking skills in the subject content areas. The academic areas of language arts and social studies/history appear particularly appropriate for combining social-emotional and academic skill development. Music, art, foreign languages, physical education, science and mathematics offer many additional opportunities for lessons that reinforce learning in the essential social-emotional competencies associated with resilience.

The parent/family component of the Developing Resilient Youth program further provides the school with a positive and constructive home-school collaboration strategy. Through DRY, parents and teachers begin working collaboratively to develop, in their children/students, the social-emotional competencies of resilient youth and subsequently to create ever more supportive home and school environments. Such supportive home and school environments are associated in the research with improved social development and higher academic achievement among youth.

The previously identified five social-emotional competencies of resilient youth form the basis for this theoretically and empirically supported model for developmental classroom guidance programs. Schools are the ideal setting for delivering such a preventive, developmental program. However, the program can easily be applied in any setting focused on fostering positive youth development. The five social-emotional competencies are intended to build upon one another and therefore can be best taught in a sequential manner during each school year. The skills of each new stage build upon those of the preceding stage. A teacher or school counselor can begin with activities to develop student skills in Understanding and Respecting Self and Others and then proceed to the subsequent skills. For each social-emotional skill lesson, follow up classroom instructional activities are suggested. The teacher is able therefore to reinforce each competency by linking it to academic instruction in the various content areas. Finally, "homework' activities are suggested which are designed to involve parents in the teaching of these essential social-emotional competency areas. Homework, in the DRY program, involves activities for parents to complete at home which reinforce the classroom lesson in a social-emotional skill area; it does not involve a task for the child to complete! Some students may need assistance in identifying a relative, school volunteer, or community mentor to participate when the parent is unable to fulfill this role.

The DRY program is intended to be repeated through each grade level in a spiraling manner such that each class group repeats the five skills but with differing, and developmentally appropriate, learning activities. This process results not only with students developing the skills and attitudes associated with personal resilience but simultaneously the classroom group evolves into an increasingly more cohesive, cooperative and supportive environment. Positive classroom climate has long been associated with improved academic achievement and decreased social and behavioral problems.

As noted by Benard (2004; 1991) in reviewing the research on resilience, optimal development in youth appears to be the result of the development of two primary processes: a) the development of the essential social-emotional competencies and b) the presence of supportive social environments of home, school and community. The Developing Resilient Youth program strives to facilitate both of these processes.

**Developing Your Classroom Program**

Specific resilience skill development activities are provided in this manual including suggested supplementary classroom and home activities for each lesson. It is suggested that teachers schedule a 30- 45 minute DRY class session at the beginning of each week. This lesson is then reinforced during the week through the supplementary academic instructional activities and the parent involvement "homework" activities. While the activities included in this manual form the basis of the program, teachers and counselors are encouraged to develop and expand upon these classroom activities by incorporating other programs and lesson plans so as to best meet the unique needs and interests of the students in their particular school and their classroom. The pre-packaged, "*one size fits all*" program model is rejected here! The Developing Resilient Youth program is intended to provide the model or framework for developing a comprehensive program appropriate to each school's unique situation, concerns and student population. The program can readily be expanded upon further and specifically tailored to each school's unique population and each teacher's unique classroom group.

Using the DRY model, additional social-emotional competence lesson plans can be readily adopted, developed and then included within each teacher's classroom program. Several resources for locating additional DRY program lessons are listed in Appendix "A'. It is important to tailor the program to your particular school and classroom needs. However, it is also important to be sure to include supplementary home activities and academic instructional activities with each classroom social-emotional learning activity. Teachers are further encouraged to work collaboratively with colleagues in other subject specialty areas so as to develop a well integrated program in the school. The social-emotional competency of Responsible Contribution is particularly open to further development and expansion in a variety of possible directions. Depending upon the school's student population and curriculum requirements, such topics as career development, substance abuse, conflict resolution, ethical decision making, sexuality education, problem solving, and community service can all be readily included under this competency area.

In all cases however, the best results are realized through the use of experiential learning activities rather than group discussion formats. It is also best to conclude each DRY classroom lesson with a brief follow-up class discussion. With younger children, the follow up discussion should be kept relatively short (maximum 10 minutes). As the age and grade level of the students increases, the ratio of experiential activity to discussion moves increasingly toward a 1:1 ratio. The teacher should end each lesson by leading the class through a five-step follow-up discussion process involving:

- **What occurred during this activity?**
- **How did you feel at the beginning, middle, and end of the activity?**
- **What did you learn from this activity?**
- **What similar situations occur in your life where you could apply this skill? OR, When was a time that this information or skill would have helped you?**
- **What might you do to use this skill in future situations?**

**Summary**

Schools, and classroom teachers in particular, can optimize their effectiveness by implementing a resiliency-based, developmental classroom guidance program consistent with the concepts of Resilience, Positive Psychology, Gemeinschaftsgefuhl (aka: Social Interest), Social-Emotional Intelligence, Character Education, and Social Skills training. The implementation of such a positive, preventive model is well supported by the empirical research on child and adolescent adjustment and school/career success. The ultimate goal of the Developing Resilient Youth classroom guidance program is to provide a "Social Vaccine" for youth; a vaccine which immunizes them from the myriad of social problems and stressors which they will encounter throughout their lives while simultaneously improving their academic achievement.

Hopefully, the Developing Resilient Youth program will assist in moving toward the creation of a truly transformative schools that provide students with both the academic and social-emotional competencies they will need to be successful in life. It is hoped that by doing so educators will fulfill the charge initially set forward centuries ago by Dr. John Phillips when, in 1781, he challenged his teachers to ensure that " . . . *the disposition of the minds and morals of the youth under their charge will exceed every other care; well considering that though goodness without knowledge is weak and feeble, yet knowledge without goodness is dangerous, and that both united form the noblest character and lay the sweet foundation of usefulness to mankind.*"

# References

Ansbacher, H. (1968). The concept of social interest. *Journal of Individual Psychology*, 2(24), 131-149.

Adler, A. (1929). *Individualpsychologie in der Schule: Vorleungen fur lehrer und erzieher*, Leipzig: Hirzel.

Barber, B. & Olsen, J. (1997). Socialization in context: Connection, regulation and autonomy in the family, school, and neighborhood, and with peers. *Journal of adolescent research*, 12, 287-315.

Benard, B. (2004). *Resiliency: what we have learned*. San Francisco, CA: WestEd publishers.

Benard, B. (1991) *Fostering resiliency in kids: Protective factors in the family, school and community*. Portland, OR: Western Regional Educational Laboratory.

California Task Force to Promote Self-Esteem and Personal and Social Responsibility (1990). *Toward a state of esteem*. Sacramento, CA: California Department of Education.

21st Century Skills (2007). Beyond the Three Rs: Voter attitudes toward 21st century skills. www.21stcenturyskills.org.

Child Trends (2008). http://www.childtrends.org/files/Child_Trends-20089_09_15_FR_Readiness.

Charters, W.W. (1922). Regulating the project. *Journal of Educational Research*, 5, 245-246.

Cohen, D.A. & Rice, J. (1997). Parenting styles, adolescent substance abuse, and academic achievement. *Journal of Drug Education, 27*(2). 199-211.

Collins, J. (2001). *Good to Great: Why some companies make the leap and others don't*. New York: Harper-Collins.

Diekstra, R.F.W. (2008). Effectiveness of school-based social and emotional learning programs worldwide. In, *Social and emotional education: An international analysis*, pp. 255-312. Santender, Spain: Fundacion Marcelino Butin.

Dornbusch, S., Ritter, P., Leiderman, P.H., Roberts, D.F. & Fraleigh, M. (1987). The relations of parenting style to adolescent school performance. *Child Development, 58*, 1244-1257.

Dweck, C.S. (2006). *Mindset: the new psychology of success*. New York: Ballentine Books.

Dweck, C.S. (2000). *Self-Theories: Their role in motivation, personality and development*. Hove, E. Sussex: Psychology Press.

Eccles, J. & Gootman, J. (2002). *Community programs to promote youth development*. Washington, DC: National Academies Press.

Goleman, D. (2006). *Social Intelligence.* New York: Bantam Books.

Goleman, D. (1995*). EQ: Why it can matter more than IQ.* New York: Bantam Books.

Johnson, D.W. & Johnson, R. T. (1989). Social skills for successful group work. *Educational Leadership, 47*(4), 29-33.

Juvonen, J & Wentzel, K. ( 1997). *Social Motivation: Understanding children's school adjustment.* Cambridge, UK: Cambridge University Press.

Katz, L. G., & McClellan, D. E. (1997). *Fostering children's social competence: The teacher's role.* Washington, DC : National Association for the Education of Young Children. ED 413 073.

King, K.P (2005). *Bringing transformative learning to life.* Malavar, FL: Krieger.

Kliebard, H.M. (1990). Success and failure in educational reform: Are there historical LESSONS? *Peabody Journal of Education*, 65, 144-157.

Kliebard, H.M. (1990). Success and failure in educational reform: Are there historical LESSONS? *Peabody Journal of Education, 65*, 144-157.

Kumpfer, K. (1999). Factors and processes contributing to resilience: The resilience framework. IN M. Glantz & J. Johnson (Eds.), *Resilience and development: Positive life adaptations.* (pp. 269-277). New York, NY: Kluwer.

Lahey, B., "Gordon, R., Loeber, R., Strouthamer-Locher, M. & Farrington, D. (1999). Boys who join gangs: A prospective study of predictors of first gang entry. *Journal of Abnormal Child Psychology, 27,* 261-276.

Libbey, H.P. (2004). Measuring student relationships to school: Attachment bonding connectedness and engagement. *Journal of school health, 74*(7), 274-283.

Maslow, A. (1964). Synergy in the society and in the individual. *Journal of Individual Psychology, 20,* 153-164.

Mayer, J.D. & Salovey, P.(1997). What is Emotional Intelligence? In, P. Salovey and D. Sluyter (Eds), *Emotional development and emotional intelligence: Implications for educators.* New York, NY: Basic Books.

McClellan, D. E., & Kinsey, S. (1999) Children's social behavior in relation to participation in mixed-age or same-age classrooms. *Early Childhood Research & Practice* [Online], 1(1). Available: http://ecrp. uiuc.edu/v1n1/v1n1.html

Mezirow, J. (2000). *Learning as transformation: Critical perspectives on a theory in progress.* San Francisco, CA: Jossey-Bass.

McNeely C and Falci, C. (2004). School connectedness and the transition into and out of health-risk behavior among adolescents: A comparison of social belonging and teacher support. *Journal of school health, 74*(7), 284-288.

Olweus, D. (1993*). Bullying at School: What we know and what we can do about it.* Oxford, UK: Blackwell

Oetting, E.R. & Beauvis, P. (1987). Peer cluster theory, socialization characteristics, and adolescent drug use: A path analysis. *Journal of Counseling Psychology*, 3-4, 205-213.

Oliner, S.P. & Oliner, P.M. (1988). *The Altruistic Personality: Rescuers of Jews in Nazi Europe.* New York: The Free Press.

Payton, J., Weissberg, R.P., Durlak, J.A., Dymnicki, A. B., Taylor, R.D., Schellinger, K.B. & Pachan, M. (2008). The positive impact of social and emotional learning for kindergarten to eighth-grade students: Findings from three scientific reviews. *Technical report, Collaborative for Academic, Social, and Emotional Learning (CASEL).* www.casel.org.

Paulson, S.E., Marchant, G.J., & Rothlisberg, B.A. (1997). Early adolescents' perceptions of patterns of parenting, teaching, and school atmosphere: Implications for achievement. *Journal of Early Adolescence, 18*, 5-12.

Resnick, M.D., Bearman, P.S., Blum, R.W., Bauman, K.E., Harris, K.M., Jones, J. et al. (1997).

Protecting adolescents from harm: Findings from the national longitudinal study on adolescent health. *Journal of the American Medical Association, 278*(10), 823-832.

Parker, J. G., & Asher, S. R. (1987). Peer relations and later personal adjustment: Are low-accepted children at risk? *Psychological Bulletin*, 102(3), 357-389.

Phillips, J. (1781). Mission statement for Phillips Academy and Phillips Exeter Academy. http://www.exeter.edu/about_us/about_us_286aspx.

Ryan, K. (1986). The new moral education. *Phi Delta Kappan*, 228-223.

Salovey, P. & Mayer, J.D. (1990). *Emotional Intelligence. Imagination, Cognition and Personality,* 9, 185-211.

Twemlow, S.W., Fonagy, P., Sacco, F.C., Gies, M.L, Evans, R & Ewbank, R (2001). Creating a peaceful school learning environment: A controlled study of an elementary school intervention to reduce violence. *American Journal of Psychiatry, 158* (5), 808-810.

Twemlo, S. W. & Sacco, F.C. (2008). *Why school anti-bullying programs don't work.* New York: Jason Aronson.

Zins, J.E., Weissberg, R.P., Wang, M.C. & Walberg, H.J. (Eds), (2004). *Building academic success thru social and emotional learning: What does the research say?* New York: Teachers College Press.

# Appendix A

# Additional Resources for Classroom Activities for your Developing Resilient Youth Curriculum

---

**Bullying Prevention:**

Olweus, D., et. al. (2009). Classroom Meetings that Matter: A year's worth of resources for grades K-5. (2009). Center City, MN: Hazeldon. www.olweus.org

Olweus, D., et. al. (2009). Classroom Meetings that Matter: A year's worth of resources for grades 6-8. Center City, MN: Hazeldon. www.olweus.org

**Heifer International:**

Projects to end hunger and poverty around the world. www.heifer.org

**Learning to Give:**

Curriculum division of The League. Provides lesson plans to teach social emotional competencies in all grade levels and subject areas. www.learningtogive.org/lessons

**Passport to Peace:**

National School of Character award winning program. For information contact:
Ana Leon, program coordinator at ana.leon@browardschools.com

**PE Central:**

Resource for PE teachers providing PE activities and games that teach children a variety of social emotional skills. www.pecentral.org/lessonideas

**Second Step:**

Lessons for School & Life by the Committee for Children organization. Full pre-school thru grade 8 curriculum. www.cfchildren.org

**Teaching Tolerance:**

A project of the southern poverty law center. www.tolerance.org

**Service Project Resources:**

Friedman, J & Roehldepartain, J. (2010), Doing Good Together: 101 easy, meaningful service projects for families, schools and communities. Minneapolis, MN: Freespirit Publishing.

**Social Emotional Learning Activities:**

Skills for Living: Group counseling activities for young adolescents. Rosemarie Smead Morganett (1990). Champaign, ILL: Research Press. www.researchpress.com/product/item/4761

Skills for Living: Group counseling activities for elementary students, Rosemarie Smead Morganett (1990). Champaign, ILL: Research Press. www.researchpress.com/product/item/4761

Resilience Builder Program for Children and Adolescents, Alford, M., Zucker, B., & Grados, J. www.researchpress.com/resilience/builder/program/item/6620

Skillstreaming the Elementary School Child. McGinnis, E., www.researchpress.com/skillstreaming/elementary/product/item/6586.

Social Decision Making/Social Problem Solving (k-8), Butler, L., Romasz-McDonald, T., & Elias, M. www.researchpress.com/product/item/6563.

I Can Problem Solve. Shure, M., www. www.researchpress.com/product/item/4628.

Promoting Alternative Thinking Strategies (PATHS). Greenberg, M. & Kusche, C., www.prevetnion.psu.edu/projects/PATHS.html.

Safe and Caring Schools. www.safeandcaringschools.com

Tribes Learning Community. www.tribes.com

# Understanding & Respecting Self and Others Skills

# *Understanding & Respecting Self & Others*

## [Grades 4 and above]

# Class Autobiographies

### Objective(s):

- To assist students in getting to know more about one another
- To promote class cohesiveness
- To assist students in finding commonalities and interesting aspects of one another

### Materials:

- Writing materials

### Lesson Plan:

*Introduction:* Discuss with the class what an autobiography is and the types of information which might be found in someone's autobiography (e.g., early life, family history, important events in one's life, interesting or fun incidents, places lived, friends, favorite activities, etc)

*Activity:* Have student write their own autobiography. Have students also make a book cover for their autobiography and bind them into a class folder (3 ring binder) as a Collection of Class ## Autobiographies. Leave time daily for anyone to read part or all of their autobiography (or the teacher may read sections from each student's autobiography to the class). Make several copies such that they can be located somewhere in the room for "free reading" time. Also, by using a 3-ring binder, students can be encouraged to add new sections at any time.

*Closure:* After a student has read a section of his/her autobiography to the class, the teacher may invite the class to respond by noting particularly interesting parts and/or to make requests for further information and/or details about their classmate's life (e.g. for developing a later chapter). Be clear that only positive comments are acceptable regarding another student's autobiography. (e.g. "I'd really like to hear more about your old neighborhood if you could write more sometime" . . . avoid, "good, but" statements as the "but" discourages further effort!).

Have the students keep their autobiographies on a selected table or bookshelf in the classroom Such that during free time, or reading/writing time, they can add to their booklets or read a classmate's autobiography. A "Comments" sheet can be included as the last page of each student's autobiography. Anytime someone reads a classmate's booklet, he or she can make some positive and encouraging comments.

## Suggested Classroom Follow-Up Activities:

- Have students read (or read to students) autobiographies of famous individuals from throughout history. Discuss how these life events may have helped form their character in later life.

- Use the autobiographies as part of an on-going class writing project encouraging students to add chapters/sections to their initial effort.

- The classroom teacher should contribute his/her own autobiography to the class book. Also invite other school staff to contribute short autobiographies (e.g. principal, counselor, custodian, bus driver, cafeteria workers, etc).

## Suggested Home Follow-Up Activities:

- Ask parents to write their own autobiographies (provide prompts and ideas to get them started) and include this in your classroom's Library; "Autobiographies of Our Parents".

- Have students invite grandparents or other elderly friends, family and neighbors to write similar autobiographies focusing on how times were different (or similar) in their childhoods and how they experienced important historical events (e.g. WWII, McCarthyism, Kennedy presidency and assassination, Civil Rights Movement and Segregation, Berlin Wall, Vietnam, Gulf War, Nixon and Watergate, etc.)

- Provide students with a selection of autobiographies from the library and ask parents to read the books to or with their child at home and discuss what they learned interesting about this person's life. (e.g. sports figures, historical figures, entertainers, etc.)

# The Four Questions

## Objective(s):

- To develop classroom cohesion through learning more about one another
- To develop skills in learning to understand one another more deeply.

## Materials:

- One page of composition paper for each group (4-5 students per group)

## Lesson Plan:

*Introduction:* Ask students if they have ever seen a person interviewed by a reporter or TV show. Who was interviewed? What was the purpose of interviews?

Inform the students that they will have an opportunity over the course of the week to interview their classmates to get to know one another at a deeper, more meaningful level.

*Activity:* Divide the class into work groups of 4-6 students each (assign a recorder for each group). Then instruct each group to come up with a list of ten questions they would like to ask you and their classmates in an interview with the goal of getting to know more about who we each are. Put the words "Who?" and "What?" on the front board. After the groups are done, inform them that interview questions can be "Who" questions which help us learn more about that person's values, beliefs, what they care most about, or finds important in his/her life (e.g. "What is something you've done that you're proud of, and why?"). "What" questions, on the other hand, tell us facts but nothing more (e.g. "age, name, address, etc). Discuss with the class the type of information each of these questions reveal. Have the groups share some of their questions and determine if they are "who" or "what" questions and list accordingly under the proper heading on the board. Invite the students to review their questions and make as many possible into "Who?" type interview questions.

Begin by having the students interview you, their teacher, by each group's recorder asking, in turn, one of their questions. State at the outset that whenever we are asked an interview question, we have two options: to answer honestly or, to respectfully decline to answer if it is too personal or inappropriate. Have each group then ask you one question and answer

*William G. Nicoll, PhD*

accordingly. After each group has asked one question repeat the cycle with their second question, etc. until each group has asked four questions

Over the course of the next week or two, schedule time each day for the interviewing of each and every student in the class. For example, interview two students each morning or 1-2 students at the beginning and ending of each school day. Have each group rotate each time in asking the questions such that everyone gets to be an interviewer as well as interviewee.

***Closure:*** Following each interview, have classmates respond to what they have learned about the interviewee by sharing a) something I learned that was interesting, or would like to know more, about this person, or b) something I have in common with this person.

## Suggested Classroom Follow-Up Activities:

- Conduct class interviews of the school principal and other school staff

- Whenever a new student joins the class, give them the opportunity to be interviewed by their classmates.

- Have students watch interviews of political figures, athletes, etc and discuss what they learn about that person's values, interests, and why he/she chooses to act and say the things they do.

- Have students read an autobiography of a famous person and then present a report in an interview format using the class questions and how they think this person would have responded.

## Suggested Home Follow-Up Activities:

- Have students interview a parent, grandparent or neighbor whom they would like to learn more about and present what they learned in class.

- Have students watch an interview Television show with a parent and then discuss what they each learned about "who" the interviewee is as a person.

- Have students complete a homework assignment in which they are to ask a parent, sibling or neighbor who they would most like to interview, if they could interview anybody living or deceased (e.g. famous historical figures). Have the adult specify what three questions they would most like to ask that person and why. Discuss in class.

| **WHAT I Am?** | **WHO I am?** |
|---|---|

**Question #1:**

**Question #2:**

**Question #3:**

**Question #4:**

# *Understanding & Respecting Self & Others*
## [All Grade Levels]

# Personal Coat-of-Arms

## Objective(s):

- To help students share and understand more about themselves and their classmates in regard to their family heritage and personal interests, values, etc.
- To develop greater class cohesion, belonging.
- To help students think more deeply regarding their values, interests and family history.

## Materials:

- Provide each student with a piece of paper with a drawing of a standard "coat-of-arms" as per attached example.
- Students will also need colored pencils for completing the coats of arms.

## Lesson Plan:

*Introduction:* Discuss with students the origins of "coats of arms" in Europe during medieval times. During those times local nobleman, kings, and so forth had armies but most "soldiers" were not professional military but rather people loyal to that king or nobleman. Often people identified more with a specific family clan or tribe. Battles were largely hand to hand combat and one could easily become disoriented. When sounding the signal to retreat and regroup, "soldiers" could easily get confused as to which side was whom. Thus, the leader could hold up his shield with the coat of arms identifying who he was so soldiers retreated to group with their respective nobleman leader. Each leader developed his own unique coat of arms which reflected things about his family, to which king or clan he was loyal to and something unique about his family heritage.

*Activity:* Have the students create their own coat-of-arms using the shield drawn on the handout paper. The coat of arms is divided into six sections. Students are instructed to illustrate their answer to each of the given six questions in the respective sections. Words are not allowed on the coat of arms but only on the banner beneath. Finally, in the banner at the bottom of the coat of arms have the students write a motto they or their family tries to live by.

*Sample Questions:*

- Something special or unique about your family.
- One thing you do or enjoy the best.
- Something special about you.
- What do you hope to be doing in 20 years from now?
- What is the one thing that makes you most happy or proud?
- The best thing you ever did.
- Something you'd like to be able to do better or know more about.
- Your favorite school subject
- Your favorite after school activity

*Closure:* Have students individually share any or all of the sections on their personal coat-of-arms with the class as they so choose. After completing their presentation, hang the coats of arms on the walls around the room indicating the "noblemen and noble women" that make up this classroom kingdom. (The teacher should complete his/her coat-of-arms also to include with the students on the wall).

## Suggested Classroom Follow-Up Activities:

- Link this activity to a social studies/history lesson of the middle ages.

- Read tales of King Arthur, or other medieval leaders.

- Have students research the coats of arms of kings, etc from throughout Europe and identify the meaning of the symbols.

## Suggested Home Follow-Up Activities:

- Have students bring home an extra coat of arms worksheet for a parent, grandparent or other family member to complete. Then share in class what their parents included in the coat of arms and why.

- Have parents assist the students to complete a family tree or genogram going back at least three generations (parents, grandparents, great-grandparents) and include information on where each lived, what they did, etc. Share any or all in class as students so choose. (the teacher should complete his or her family tree or genogram also.

- Have parents write a favorite family story about a family ancestor (e.g. grandparent, great grandparent, great aunt/uncle, etc). Ask parents to read it to their child and discuss why that story is important to them. Then have the students make a book of "Our Family Stories" and make available for students' free reading time.

# <u>Personal Coat of Arms</u>

## Personal Coat of Arms

------------

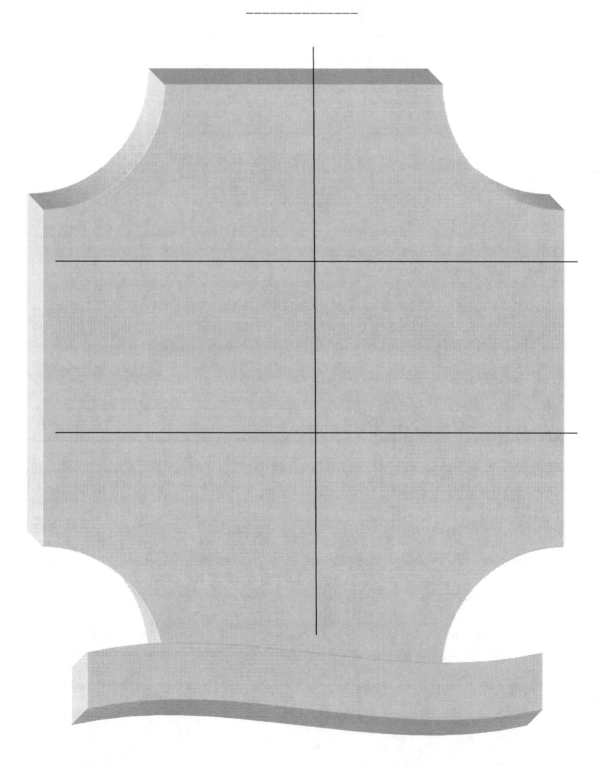

[All Grade Levels]

# Personal Inventory

## Objective(s):

- To assist students in gaining a greater understanding of their individual similarities and differences.
- To develop increased classroom cohesion and sense of belonging among all students.

## Materials:

Personal Inventory sheets for each student and the teacher (attached)

## Lesson Plan:

*Introduction:* Explain to the students that this activity is intended to help them get to know one another better. Briefly discuss how it feels to be with people who know you well, e.g., friends and family, versus being a stranger in a large group. Share experiences of the latter.

*Activity:* Have the students complete the Personal Inventory Questionnaire on their own. Then allow time for the students to go about the room sharing their responses with classmates. For each question, students should write in the names of at least two others in the class who answered the same as he/she did. The teacher should join in this activity. Ask if there were any questions for which you could not find a classmate with the same answer. Check with the class to see if anyone actually did answer the same. Otherwise, note that this is something unique to this student. See which questions had the greatest percentage of "same answers" by having students who answered the same way all stand up; then have them sit and check out the numbers with other answers.

*Closure:* Ask the students to share how they felt during the activity at the beginning and then at the end. Discuss the advantages of meeting people like oneself as well as meeting people who are different. What does each add to our lives?

## Suggested Classroom Follow-Up Activities:

- Have students share what they liked about the books they read and enjoyed and why.

- Create "literary clubs" in the class where students with similar interests can read the same book together and share what they liked or disliked.

- Invite students to discuss their responses to "what I dislike about school" in a problem solving format . . . i.e., "How could we work to improve this part of school?"

- Provide an opportunity for students answering the "career field interested in?" question to explore that career together as a group and make a report to the class (and/or invite in a quest speaker in that field . . . parent, community member, etc)

## Suggested Home Follow-Up Activities:

- Have students ask their parents to make out the inventory and then compare parent's responses among those of classmate's parents. (change word "school" to "work or job".)

- Ask parents to read their favorite book to their child and share what they like about the story.

- Ask parents to share (i.e., read to) their favorite children's story (fable, fairytale, etc) from their childhood with their child. Have the parents briefly write why they liked the story and which character was their favorite and why. Students can then share this in class. [Note: can also be done with favorite movies, tv show, etc from their childhood and share with their son/daughter]

# PERSONAL INVENTORY

Fill in your answer underneath each of the questions below. Then find at least two classmates who gave the same answer and fill in their names in the space next to the question.

**NAME**: _____

1.  Color of your hair?                                                    _____
                                                                            _____

2.  Color of your eyes?                                                    _____
                                                                            _____

3.  Your favorite food?                                                    _____
                                                                            _____

4.  Your favorite TV Show?                                                 _____
                                                                            _____

5.  Your favorite color?                                                   _____
                                                                            _____

6.  An activity you enjoy outside of school?                               _____
                                                                            _____

7.  A career field (job) you are interested in?                            _____
                                                                            _____

8.  Your favorite book that you've read and enjoyed?                       _____
                                                                            _____

9.  What do you like best about school?                                    _____
                                                                            _____

10. What do you like least about school?                                   _____
                                                                            _____

# Friendship Books

## Objective:

To assist students in recognizing characteristics of a friendly relationship and to teach them to identify and plan an activity that shows good friendship skills and appreciation of another.

## Materials:

Chalkboard, newsprint, overhead projector, chalk, marker, overhead pen, and worksheet on, "Things a Good Friend Does".

## Lesson:

*Introduction:* Ask the class, "Why are friends important?" "How many have or had a best friend?". Then have the class list "famous friendships we all know about" and list on the board:

e.g., Pooh and Piglet, Charlotte and Wilbur, etc.

*Activity:*

*Step 1.* Let's brainstorm a list of what makes a person a good friend (make list on chalkboard, newsprint or overhead).

*Step 2.* Now let's think of some things friends DO for each other that make us want them for our friend. (Again, list on responses on the board, newsprint or overhead).

*Step 3.* Wow! It sounds like friends are really important! Let's think about what each of us can do this week to be a good friend to someone and let them know that we really care about them and appreciate their friendship (accept a few suggestions).

*Step 4.* Those are some good ideas to get us thinking. Let's each take a few minutes to develop a plan something special we could do this week to be a good friend and let someone know how much we appreciate their friendship. Write your plan on the worksheet I'm passing out to each of you now. You may also draw a picture of you and your friend when you are implementing your plan and being a good and special friend. We will then put all our ideas into a special book to keep in class on "How to be a Good Friend".

*Closure:*

Begin with a sharing of students' picture stories, "OK, let's share some of the ideas we've come up with on how to be a good friend". After a few share their ideas, collect the student's worksheets and create a bookbinder organizing their worksheets into a booklet format. Let the students know it will be left in the reading area of the room for students to look at during the week.

How many think you will use some of these ideas this week to be a good friend to someone?@

Try to think about other things you can do all the time, or something your friend has done that makes them a special friend. Let students know you will leave out extra worksheets to that as they come up with new ideas we can add them to the Friendship Book.

## Suggested Classroom Follow-up Activities:

• Post several quotes from the "Friendship Quotes" list below and have students write a short essay or journal entry on their favorite quote and what it means to them.

• Have the students research great friendships in history and literature (e.g. Thomas Edison and Henry Ford; Tom Sawyer and Huck Finn) and how these friendships affected them.

• Discuss International Friendship Day (August 1st) and research how it was founded and is now celebrated around the world.

• Have students read the Anna Cummins quote: "Do not save your loving speeches For your friends till they are dead; Do not write them on their tombstones, Speak them rather now instead. Then have each write a letter to a friend telling them what the appreciate most about them as a friend."

• Choose stories in your instructional reading program or for reading to the class which deal with friendships; e.g., Charlotte's Web or Tom Sawyer. Or, watch a video with great friends such as Shrek & Donkey or Forrest & Bubba.

• Create an "I Spy" Bulletin Board. The bulletin board can have a pirate ship and crow's nest with lookout's spyglass or just a large eye looking out. Then place the "I Spied a True Friend" theme at the top. Throughout the week (usually after school) place note cards at the end a string running from the spyglass with the names of students whom you, the teacher, have observed displaying good friendship skills that day along with a very brief notation on the specific behavior observed. Strive to add new examples each evening such that each student is recognized for a specific behavior by the week's end.

## **Suggested Home Follow-up Activities:**

- Have parents make a list with their child of "Our Family's Friends" and next to each person note what everyone most enjoys or likes about that person; i.e., what makes him/her a special family friend.

- Have the parents brainstorm with all family members the qualities they each look for in a friend and send the list to school to make up a combined list from all the families.

- Have students bring home the Friendship Quotes and have each parent or family member choose their favorite and state why it is their favorite. Write down the quotes and reasons and bring to class for discussion/sharing.

- Have each student interview a parents regarding "Who is your best friend?" and what do they do that makes them special to you? Students can share their parent responses answers in class the next day.

- With the assistance of your librarian, suggest a list of books to parents that involve friendship which they could read with their children this week.

- Ask parents to write a short description of things their son/daughter has done to be a special friend to someone over the years. Students or the teacher can read these in class.

# Friendship Quotes

––––––––––––

"Tell me what company thou keepst, and I'll tell thee what thou art." - *Miguel de Cervantes (1547 - 1616) Spanish novelist.*

"Have no friends not equal to yourself." - *Confucious (551 - 497 BC).*

"A friend is a person with whom I may be sincere. Before him I may think aloud." - *Ralph Waldo Emerson*

"The only reward of virtue is virtue; the only way to have a friend is to be one." - *Ralph Waldo Emerson*

"It is one of the blessings of old friends that you can afford to be stupid with them." - *Ralph Waldo Emerson*

"True happiness consists not in the multitude of friends, but in their worth and choice." - *Samuel Johnston, (as above)*

"Associate yourself with men of good quality if you esteem your own reputation; for 'tis better to be alone than in bad company." - *George Washington (1732 - 1799)*

"I can never think of promoting my convenience at the expense of a friend's interest and inclination." - *George Washington,*

"It is not so much our friends' help that helps us as the confident knowledge that they will help us." - *Epicurus (341 - 270 BC) Greek philosopher.*

"It is not so much our friends' help that helps us as the confident knowledge that they will help us." - *Epicurus*

"Sir, I look upon every day to be lost, in which I do not make a new acquaintance." - *Samuel Johnston, (as above)*

"To like and dislike the same things, that is indeed true friendship." - *Sallust (86 - 334 BC) Roman historian*

"One loyal friend is worth ten thousand relatives." - *Euripides, Greek playwright*

"My friends are my estate." - *Emily Dickinson*

*William G. Nicoll, PhD*

"Be slow to fall into friendship; but when thou art in, continue firm and constant." - *Socrates, Greek Philosopher*

"Friendship is the only cement that will ever hold the world together" - *Woodrow Wilson*

"Anybody can sympathize with the sufferings of a friend, but it requires a very fine nature to sympathize with a friend's success." - *Oscar Wilde*

"Friendship with oneself is all-important because without it one cannot be friends with anyone else in the world." - *Eleanor Roosevelt*

"If you judge people, you have no time to love them." - *Mother Teresa*

"I will speak ill of no man, and speak all the good I know of everybody." - *Benjamin Franklin*

"Misfortune shows those who are not really friends." - *Aristotle*

"The bird a nest,
the spider a web,
man friendship." - *William Blake*

"Never injure a friend, even in jest." - *Cicero*

"A true friend stabs you in the front." - *Oscar Wilde*

"Think where man's glory most begins and ends, and say my glory was I had such friends." - *William Yeats*

"Grief can take care of itself, but to get the full value of joy you must have somebody to divide it with." - *Mark Twain*

"The best mirror is an old friend." - *George Herbert*

"What is a friend? A single soul in two bodies." - *Aristotle*

"The friendship that can cease has never been real." - *Saint Jerome*

"I count myself in nothing else so happy
As in a soul remembering my good friends." - *William Shakespeare*

"Too late we learn, a man must hold his friend un-judged, accepted, trusted to the end." - *John Boyle O'Reilly*

"Without friends no one would choose to live, though he had all other goods." - *Aristotle*
"My best friend is the one who brings out the best in me." - *Henry Ford*

"The making of friends, who are real friends, is the best token we have of a man's success in life." - *Edward Everett Hale*

"Except in cases of necessity, which are rare, leave your friend to learn unpleasant things from his enemies; they are ready enough to tell them." - *Oliver Wendell Holmes*

"The most I can do for my friend is simply to be his friend. I have no wealth to bestow on him. If he knows that I am happy in loving him, he will want no other reward. Is not friendship divine in this?" - *Henry David Thoreau*

"Friendship that flows from the heart cannot be frozen by adversity, as the water that flows from the spring cannot congeal in winter." - *James Fenimore Cooper*

"Friendship without self interest is one of the rare and beautiful things in life." - *James Francis Byrnes*

"Friendship is the only thing in the world concerning the usefulness of which all mankind are agreed." - *Cicero*

"Walking with a friend in the dark is better than walking alone in the light." - *Helen Keller*

"Happiness is time spent with a friend and looking forward to sharing time with them again." - *Lee Wilkinson*

"Ah, how good it feels . . . the hand of an old friend" - *Mary Englebright*

"Never injure a friend, even in jest." - *Cicero*

". . . no man is useless
while he has a friend." - *Robert Louis Stevenson*

"Be slow in choosing your friends; slower in changing." -*Benjamin Franklin*

"Go often to the house of thy friend, for weeds choke the unused path." -*Ralph Waldo Emerson, American writer and philosopher (1803-1882)*

"'Stay' is a charming word in a friends vocabulary." -*Louisa Mary Alcott [1832-1888], American writer, reformist*

"When we seek to discover the best in others, we somehow bring out the best in ourselves." -*William Arthur Ward*

"In the end, we will remember not the words of our enemies, but the silence of our friends." - *Martin Luther King Jr.*

# The Courage to Succeed

## Objective(s):

- Help students identify "fear of failure" responses in their lives
- Encourage students to maintain courage when faced with failure or frustration
- Help students identify strategies for persevering and ultimate success

## Materials:

- Writing journals
- Book: "The book of heroic failures" by Stephen Pile (Penguin Readers by Pearson Education, 2000).

## Lesson Plan:

*Introduction:* Read one of the tales of Heroic Failure from the book, The Book of Heroic Failures. Ask students why they think the author calls these stories, "heroic failures'.

*Activity:* Tell your students a true story about a time you tried something and failed. Ask students if they have ever tried something and it did not come out well, or they failed? Share experiences we have all had with failure. Then ask students to brainstorm (and list on blackboard) all the techniques we have learned to use to avoid doing things in school when we are not sure of our ability to be correct or successful (e.g. look at the floor, avoid eye contact with teacher, go to bathroom, get stomach ache, etc.).

*Closure:* Invite students to now create a second list of things we can do to help ourselves and classmates when we or they are struggling with something in school. Make a list and post in the room about "How Our Class Instills the Courage to Succeed".

## Suggested Classroom Follow-Up Activities:

- Assign each student or small group of students to research the biographies of famous individuals who struggled in school but later achieved success (e.g. Winston Churchill, Abraham Lincoln, G.K. Chesterton, Thomas Edison, Pablo Picasso, Henry Ford, James Watt, Albert Einstein, Steven Spielberg, Isaac Newton, Giaccomo Puccini, John Cheever,

John Lennon, Lucian Pavarotti, Jerry Lewis, Orville Wright, and so forth.). Have students share and post their reports to the class.

- Put the famous quotes by Winston Churchill's, "Success is going from failure to failure with undiminished enthusiasm" and Thomas Edison, "none of my experiments ever failed, I just happened to discover thousands of things that do not work". Then, invite the students to think about "What I would do if I knew I could not fail". Have the students write their stories in their journals. Afterward, invite students to share their stories.

- Allow students to read the short stories in the Book of Heroic Failures and write about which story they liked best and why.

- Read some of the quotes from the chapter on "the Art of Being Wrong". Have students write a short essay as if they were the person who made the quote and why they believed their statement to be correct.

## Suggested Home Follow-Up Activities:

- Invite parents to relate (or write) a short story about a time they tried and failed at something. Include what people did that was helpful (encouraging) or hurtful (discouraging) at that time.

- Have parents relate (or write) a short story about someone who encouraged and helped them when they were struggling in school or at work.

- Have parents (or grandparents) make a list of the things we have now that, when they were young seemed impossible or science fiction ideas only. Then have the student and parent list five things for the future that people think impossible now. Share these in class.

# **Art of Being Wrong**

"Flight by machines heavier than air is unpractical and insignificant, if not utterly impossible." Simon Newcomb (1835-1909) statement published 18 months prior to Wright brother's first flight.

"Rail travel at high speed is not possible, because passengers, unable to breathe, would die of asphyxia". Dr. Dionysys Lardner (1793-1850), professor of natural philosophy and astronomy, University College, London.

"Steamboats will never be able to cross the Atlantic since it would require more coal than it could possibly carry". Dr. Dionysys Lardner (1793-1850), professor of natural philosophy and astronomy at University College, London. Just two years later the Great Western steam ship crossed the Atlantic Ocean.

"Animals, which move, have limbs and muscles. The earth does not have limbs and muscles; therefore it does not move". Scipio Chiaramonti.

"I can accept the theory of relativity as little as I can accept the existence of atoms and other such dogmas". Ernst Mach (1838 – 1916), professor of physics, University of Vienna.

"We don't like their sound. groups of guitars are on the way out." Decca Recording Company when turning down a British rock group called, The Beatles, in 1962.

"You will never amount to very much" A Munich schoolmaster to a struggling ten year old student in his class named, Albert Einstein.

"You can't sing, you have no voice at all". A music teacher's comment to a boy named, Mario Caruso.

"The energy produced by the breaking down of the atom is a very poor kind of thing. Anyone who expects a source of power from the transformation of these atoms is talking moonshine". Ernest Rutherford (1871- 1937) regarding his successful experiment to split the atom for the first time.

"Rembrandt is not to be compared in the painting of character with our extraordinarily gifted English artist, Mr. Rippingille". John Hunt (1775-1848).

"Stop wasting time by sending him for music lessons, your son has absolutely no musical talent whatsoever." Music teacher for young Italian boy named, Giaccomo Puccini.

# Understanding and Respecting Yourself and Others

## [All Grade Levels]

# Appreciating our Differences

### Objective(s):

- Students will appreciate and respect the cultural diversity of our classroom, school and/or country
- Students will explore their own cultural heritage.

### Materials:

- Photos of people of diverse racial and cultural backgrounds from around the globe
- World map and stick pins

### Lesson Plan:

*Introduction:* Begin by having students indicate what cultural/ethnic nationalities constitute their personal heritage. List these on the board and place a pin on the map indicating the nationalities represented in your class.

*Activity:* Working in small groups, have students answer following questions:

- For each race/ethnic/cultural/national group listed, identify what similarities you share and what differences there are between you?
- What activities do we all share despite our racial/cultural/religious backgrounds?
- How have other cultures brought color to your life (music, food, inventions or discoveries, celebrations, etc? What would your life be missing if you never came across a different culture?
- Discuss with the class their responses to these questions.

### Suggested Classroom/Academic Follow-Up Activities:

- Have students research their culture more fully and develop a portfolio (3 ring binder) with information such as: a) brief history of your family's country(s) of origin, b) traditional dress/clothing, c) A traditional food and it's recipe, d) five major cities or regions of their home nation, d) nation's flag, e) a special holiday festival or celebration, tradition from their country. f) Important persons or events from their native land and g) phrases from their native language such as for: peace, hello, goodbye, how are you?, thank you, please, and what is your name?. Also include at least one traditional phrase or saying from their country of origin. Go to http://babelfish.altavista.com/tr to translate words and phrases. Place the completed portfolios around the room for all to look through and share.

- Assign email pen pals from different parts of the world (or different regions of the country) and have them follow-up with each other throughout the year.

- Invite parents from different cultures to share a typical food from their culture/country and share some of the history and customs. This can also be scheduled throughout the year as each country's special holidays or traditions are recognized and celebrated in the classroom.

## Suggested Home Follow-Up Activities:

- Have students and their parents go out to eat and do a little research on what food(s) they ate, the history of the food and where it comes from originally.

- Have parents take their child to a cultural experience outside their own (e.g. church service, cultural festival, ethnic neighborhood for dinner, etc) and write a brief description of what they did and what they learned as a family.

- Have parents or grandparents share a brief story about their memories of life in their country of origin as children and how life has changed (or not changed) over the years.

### [All Grade Levels]

# Families: Similarities & Differences

## Objective(s):

- To develop an understanding of different family structures
- To develop an understanding of how families differ around the world
- To develop a greater understanding and appreciation of their own families

## Materials:

- "Our Family History" handout sheets for each student
- Blackboard or newsprint sheets

## Lesson Plan:

*Introduction:* Inform the students that today we are going to learn more about families and how they are both similar and different around the world as well as how family life changes over the generations. Begin by asking the students to brainstorm a definition for "A FAMILY". Challenge the students to consider various possible family structures.

*Activity:* Read the list (below) describing various family organizational structures. For each category have students stand if this description fits their family (you may need to define some terms such as half-sibling vs step sibling). Invite students to look around and see the classmates who have similar and different family structures. Invite students to share a little about their families on these various topics

*Stand if:*

- If you have one or more brothers
- If you have one or more sisters
- If you have both brothers and sisters
- If you have no brothers/sisters (i.e. only child)
- If you have a sibling who does not live with you
- If you have a step-brother or sister
- If you have a half-brother or sister
- If you were adopted
- If you have an adopted sibling
- If you live with both of your biological parents

- If you now or ever lived with a step-parent
- If you now or ever lived with just one parent (single parent family)
- If you now or ever had a grand-parent living with you.
- If you've ever had another person other than parents and siblings living in your home
- If your extended family (aunts/uncles, cousins, etc) all or mostly live in the same town/area.
- If your extended family lives in different states? countries?
- If your grandparents live in the same town? state? country as you do?
- If your grandparents live in a different town? state? country than you?
- If you have extended family members who live on a farm? own a store? live in a city?

***Closure:*** Invite students to share what they have learned from today's activity. Inform the students that we will be learning and sharing more about families over the coming weeks. Give each student a copy of the "Our Family History" worksheet to complete with their parents tonight and bring to class tomorrow.

## Suggested Classroom Follow-Up Activities:

- Read to, or have students read, stories about the lives of children and families in other cultures and discuss in social studies class. (culture can include ethnicity, nationality, rural/farming, inner city, international (TCK), SES (poverty vs. affluent), etc.

- Invite parents to provide mini-lessons regarding their family culture

- Assign student groups to research daily family life at different times in history: e.g., 15th century Europe or Asia, Colonial America, Massai Tribes of E. Africa, Berber Nomads, Indigenous tribes of S. America, Moslem and Hindu family life, Chinese rural family life, etc. Have groups present their research and a visual display describing/illustrating their topic.

## Suggested Home Follow-Up Activities:

- Have the parents complete the "Our Family History" worksheets and then let students share what they learned about their family and their parents or grandparents from this homework.

- Invite parents to volunteer to come in and share a family tradition with the entire class. (schedule one or two per week).

- Invite parents to share a part of their culture with the class via food, clothing, dance/music, traditional holiday celebration, etc.

# **Handout**

# *OUR FAMILY HISTORY*

*[Have your parents write in answers to each question after discussing the questions with you]*

1.  Ask your father and mother to each describe what their family life was like when they were a child.

2.  Ask your father and mother to each tell you what they know about the childhood experiences of their own mother or father (i.e. grandparents) . . . or ask grandparent directly if possible.

3.  Discuss with your parents what are some of the ways we express love and caring for one another in our family beyond just saying it? How do we SHOW we love and care for one another?

4.  What are some of your family's special traditions? This can include just special things you do together on a regular basis that is fun and enjoyable or ways you celebrate certain special holidays, occasions, etc.

5.  Please indicate below what you would be willing to come into class to share with us about your family and/or culture: (the teacher will then contact you to schedule an appropriate time for you to share this part of your family's unique heritage and culture with the class).

# Empathy Skills

## [All Grade Levels]

# Fractured Fairy Tales

**Objective(s):**

- To develop students ability to view situations from multiple perspectives, empathize.
- To stimulate creative thinking skills
- To help students empathize with other's perspectives in conflictual situations.

**Materials:**

- Any book with a famous fairytale(s).
- Writing paper

**Lesson Plan:**

*Introduction:* Read to the class the story of "Little Red Riding Hood". Then, read the Fractured Fairytale of the "The Maligned Wolf" (attached).

*Activity:* Divide the class into groups of 3-4 students. Provide the groups with a book of Famous fairytales; fairytales with which everyone is familiar and for which there is a clear "good guy" and "villain" depicted (e.g., Cinderella, Three Billy Goats Gruff, Hansel & Gretel, etc). NOTE: If your students have not been exposed to the classic fairy tales, read several to them (or use for reading lessons) over a 2-3 day period prior to this activity. Have each group choose a fairy tale and then write a "Fractured Fairy Tale" re-telling the story from the perspective of the "villain".; that is, what his side of the story might be. After the groups have completed their creative stories, or Fractured Fairy Tales, have each read their story to the class. Later, bind the stories into a class reading book for free reading time activities.

*Closure:* Discuss with the class times when they've felt misunderstood, wrongly accused or felt nobody would listen to their side of the story/conflict. Ask, "why is it important to hear both sides when there is a conflict?".

## Suggested Classroom Follow-Up Activities:

- Have students bring in newspaper articles regarding national and international issues and discuss the varying positions on each side.

- Divide the class into debate teams of 4-6 persons. Then have various team pairs research a current or historical issue (e.g. abolitionists vs pro-slavery; American rebels vs. Tories in 1776, Suffrage, WWI involvement vs. neutrality, Palestine vs Israel, etc.). Hold a classroom debate on these topics with time for observers to note the key legitimate concerns of each team's position.

- Discuss classroom readings in terms of the feelings and position of each person involved (e.g., read "Bully of Barkham Street" and discuss the feelings/issues of the bully, his victims and classmates.

## Suggested Home Follow-Up Activities:

- Have parents write a story about a time when they felt misunderstood or not heard and how they handled the situation. Have students share these stories in class.

- Have students write their own "Fractured Fairy Tales" with parental/family assistance to add to the class book.

- Have students read newspaper articles, news magazine stories or watch the tv news regarding conflicts (between nations, political parties, labor/management, etc) and discuss with their parents the various sides, or positions, of the issue. Have each student write a brief synopsis of the issue and the opposing positions and rationales for each position.

## <u>The Maligned Wolf</u>

Hello boys and girls. I came today to share with you my sad story. You see, I am not really the person you see standing before you this morning. Rather, I am in disguise. I have had to disguise my true identity for years; quite unfairly I might add. The secret is that I am actually the Wolf who used to live in a forest far, far away. But, due to a most unfortunate incident one day, I have been forced to live in hiding, disguised to protect my safety. Would you believe that today, young children are taught in schools and by their parents that I am a Bad Wolf, an evil Wolf; and it is simply not true! Let me tell you my story.

It all started one bright spring morning. It was my job, as the largest animal in the forest, to keep watch and make sure the forest remained a safe, peaceful place for all the smaller animals. On this particular morning, I was cleaning up a campsite. Some careless campers had left their campfire still smoldering which could have led to a forest fire. They also had left quite a lot of litter about their camping spot which was not good for the environment. So I set about putting dirt on the smoldering embers and picking up their carelessly left litter.

Suddenly, I caught a glimpse of a stranger coming up the pathway. I hid behind a tree to see who it might be and to make sure it was not someone up to, well. "no good" if you know what I mean. After all, it is my job to protect the smaller, defenseless animals of the forest. This stranger seemed to be quite mysterious and acted as if he or she didn't want to be recognized. This made me a bit concerned and a tad bit frightened I'm not afraid to admit. This person wore a long red cape with a big hood over the head so nobody could see who it was. And, this person was carrying a mysterious basket with a cloth covering it so as to hide whatever was in the basket. "A terrorist with a bomb" was my first thought. I had to do something, and quick.

So, in spite of my fears and without concern for my personal safety, I jumped out from behind the tree and stopped this "terrorist". "Who are you? And where are do you think you're going with that mysterious covered basket?" I asked.

Well, as it turns out, it was a young girl . . . maybe 12 or 13. She gave me some song and dance about going to her grandmother's house at the other side of the forest. She said her grandmother was ill and she was bringing some goodies for her to eat. I checked the basket and sure enough it was full of tea, chicken soup and other goodies for her grandmother. I tried to explain to her that she needs to be more aware of how she acts and dresses when going through the forest. I told her she looked and acted like a terrorist up to some evil act and it would frighten the small, defenseless animals that lived here. But, this little girl seemed to not care less. She gave me an attitude, you know, rolling eyes, big sigh, etc., etc . . . And with that she went on her way.

I decided this little girl needs to be taught a lesson about being aware of her environment and how her behavior affected others. So I took a short cut through the forest and arrived at her grandmother's house ahead of her. Her grandmother being a forest dweller herself, understood my position when I explained the situation to her. Together, we came up with the idea of playing a little trick on little miss red riding hood in order to teach her an important lesson.

So grandmother hid in the closet while I dressed up in her nightgown and nightcap and then laid in the bed pretending to me grandmother. Very soon, in came Little Miss Red Riding hood, (without even politely knocking on the door first, I might add). She said something about bringing some goodies to eat that her mother had prepared. But then, quickly added, "Oh grandma, what terribly big eyes you have". Now, do you start to see what kind of girl she really was? Not two minutes into her sick grandmother's house and she's making nasty, critical comments about her grandmother's eyes! Unbelievable! Well, I always was taught to "make lemonade from lemons" so I tried to nicely deflect this criticism by saying, "All the better to see you with my dear". Not bad, uh?!

But, what did this little deary do next? She fired off yet a second insult at who she thought was her poor, old, sick grandmother, What awfully big ears you have, grandma". Now, I think we are all seeing that this little girl was not such a nice, considerate person at all.

Imagine, not two minutes in the door and twice insulting your own grandmother. But, again I tried to make this positive by replying, "all the better to hear you with my dear". I thought surely this would be the end of her insults. But, no!!! The next words out of her mouth are yet a third insult. "Oh, grandma, what big, ugly teeth you have!"

Ok, now this is where I lost it. I know I should have handled this better and not blown my top. But this kid was so self-centered and insulting; even to whom she thought was her own sickly grandmother. You have to understand that I come from a very poor wolf family. My parents could not afford to take me to the orthodontist for braces, retainers and so forth when I was young. I've always been quite self conscious about my large, uneven teeth. So this comment just hit me where it hurts the most. I jumped out of the bed and yelled, "All the better to eat you with!!"

Now, let's face it. This is a dumb statement! Everyone knows wolves don't eat people. But this kid just started screaming and throwing a right good "Hissy fit" right there in the cabin; running from room to room screaming. At this point, I calmed down and tried to explain to her what was really going on, but that just seemed to make matters worse and she only screamed louder.

Just then, the door burst open and this huge, burly lumberjack came flying into the room with his axe, screaming that he'd save her. Never, did he even bother to ask, "What's the problem?" No, I knew right away I was in big trouble. The girl screaming hysterically; me, a wolf, chasing her and this gung-ho lumberjack smashing his way through the door like some Rambo dude to save the day. I knew this was not going to end well!

The lumberjack swung that axe and split me open across the middle. I fell to the floor and decided to act as if I were dead. When the lumberjack went over to calm the girl down, I slowly crept out the door and crawled back to my den. It took weeks to heal. And to this day, everyone is told that I am the bad guy, the Big Bad Wolf . . . Nobody has ever asked to hear my side of the story!! Has that ever happened to you??

By the way, I've still not forgiven that grandmother for staying in the closet. Why didn't' she come out when things went bad and help me? I still don't understand her just standing there and "not getting involved". If only she had stepped up and said something, this whole bad situation could have been avoided.

Well, that's my story. To this day, I have to go around disguised as the person you see before you today. Children everywhere are taught that I'm a dangerous, evil person. Who knows what they'd do to me if they found out I was the much maligned wolf from the untrue story of Little Red Riding Hood. Thanks for listening to my sad tale; I appreciate your taking the time to listen to my side of the story. Nobody else ever has!

## *Empathy Skills*
### [All Grades]

# Feelings We All Have

**Objective(s):**

- To assist students in identifying emotions they and everyone experience
- To assist students in understanding how others feel in given situations

**Materials:**

- Magazines and newspapers with pictures of people in a variety of life situations
- scissors
- Response sheets for each student with the questions listed below for the activity.

**Lesson Plan:**

*Introduction:* Discuss with the students that we all experience the full range of emotions/ feelings in our lives. However, different people may experience similar or different feelings in the same situation. Begin by having the students brainstorm all the emotions they have experienced and list on the board.

*Activity:* Divide the class into work groups of 4-6 students each. Show the class pictures of people expressing various emotions which you have cut from the magazines and newspapers, one at a time. For each picture, invite the groups to discuss and present a plausible answer to the following questions:

- How is this person feeling?
- What clues do you see to lead you to this guess?
- Why might she/he feel this way?
- What do you expect he or she will do next?
- When have you felt the same way? why?
- What did you do and how did it turn out?
- Would you handle the situation in the same way or differently now? If so, How?

*Closure:* Have the class identify from the original list on the front board those emotions which are positive/pleasant and those which are negative/unpleasant. Then, discuss with the students they find helpful versus unhelpful when they see you experiencing these emotions.

53

*William G. Nicoll, PhD*

## Suggested Classroom Follow-Up Activities:

- Have students discuss or write about characters in their reading assignments (books, stories) and/or people and events in history class. How do you think they are feeling at this moment? Why might they feel that way? How would you feel?

- Invite community members, parents who have lived through important world and local events to speak to the class about that time and how they and others felt (e.g. during segregation, Vietnam or WWII wars, death or loss of loved one, emergency rescues, etc).

- For a writing assignment (e.g. daily writing journals), have students write about "A time I felt . . ." and assign various emotions we all have experienced.

## Suggested Home Follow-Up Activities:

- Have parents write a brief essay on, "A time I felt proud of my son/daughter" and "The time I felt most scared or worried in my life". Have students share their parent's responses in class.

- Have students complete –with parental assistance - their own scrapbook of emotions (using photos, magazine/newspaper pictures etc) of people expressing a wide range of emotions. Have them label each emotion in their scrapbook.

- Have each student interview a family member(s) and list what makes each feel: happy, proud, worried, angry, hurt, loved, rejected, capable, inept, etc . . . Discuss in class and look for similarities and differences in how people feel.

## [All Grade Levels]

# Empowering Others

**Objective:**

To assist students in recognizing how others think and feel in different situations and to differentiate constructive/empowering versus destructive/overpowering responses to others.

**Materials:**

- Worksheet : *"How would you feel, think & act?"*

**Lesson:**

*Introduction:* Read the following: A young 8 year old boy, Gilbert, is struggling in the third grade at his school both socially and academically. Gilbert is essentially a non-reader still struggling with books at a beginning first grade level. Somewhat obese and socially unpopular, Gilbert tends to sit by himself and avoids school work and interactions with his classmates. He is usually daydreaming or otherwise non-attentive and off-task during class time. One of his teachers said to him in a moment of frustration, "Gilbert if we opened up your head we would not find a brain but merely a lump of white fat".

*Discuss:* How do you think Gilbert thinks and feels about himself, school, his classmates? How do you think Gilbert felt after his teacher's comments? What might he then be thinking about himself, school work, his classmates? What might a classmate do or say to help Gilbert? To make matters worse for Gilbert?

*Activity:*

Step 1: Discuss with the class the need for understanding how another person thinks and feels. Ask:

- Recall a time when someone said something hurtful or unkind.
- How did you feel/think about that individual?
- What would you have preferred they had said or done to be helpful to you?
- How would you have felt/thought about them if they had done so?
- "Why is it important to understand other people's thoughts and feelings?"

- "What might happen if we didn't show people that we understand how they feel and what they are thinking?"

*Step 2*:  Have students work in groups of three. Show students a series of photos of various students in differing academic and social situations. Have each group identify on the Group's "How would you feel/think/act?" worksheet what they think the student in the photo is feeling at the moment, why he/she might feel that way and, what he or she might be thinking.

Step 3: For each photo, have the groups then complete on their worksheet what comments and actions by classmates would be most constructive and helpful in this situation.

***Closure:*** Begin by sharing the various group's responses on the worksheets. Which of these responses do you feel would be most helpful?. How would you feel about someone you observed making such a comment? What destructive things do you commonly see others make in similar situations? Why do you suppose they feel it necessary to make such destructive, hurtful comments?

<u>*Ask:*</u>    Does anybody know what ever happened to Gilbert? It's a true story; his real name was Gilbert Keith Chesterton. Who knows who G.K. Chesterton was? (famous British author). What do you suppose turned his life around?

<u>*A*nswer</u>:  In his early teens, Gilbert was befriended by a caring older student who enjoyed books and read to/with him, encouraged him and thus inspired a love of literature.

## Suggested Classroom Follow-up Activities:

- Teachers should make a special effort to recognize and list someplace in the room constructive, caring comments and behaviors observed this week in class.

- Develop a volunteer tutor sign-up sheet to work with younger, struggling students.

- Assign for reading biographies on famous individuals who struggled but benefited from the kind, considerate and empowering acts of others: e.g., Thomas Alva Edison, Giaccomo Puccini, Brian Piccolo (Brian's Song), Sir Isaac Newton, Albert Einstein, Charles Darwin, etc . . . . Have students write reports on the books identifying feelings of main character and examples of understanding, caring and empowering acts by others.

- Music: listen to, learn and discuss songs such as "Wind beneath my wings", "Lean on Me", etc.

- Have students research G.K. Chesterton and his books, plays, etc. Read in class.

## Suggested Home Follow-up Activities:

- Have students interview their parents or another family member regarding, "Who in your life has encouraged you, lifted you up when you were down?" Have the parents (or student) write a short story describing such an incident or person from their life.

- Suggest to parents a "family movie night assignment" in which the family is to watch together and discuss a movie involving caring, empowering acts: e.g., Rudy, Brian's Song, Finding Neverland, Play it Forward, etc.

- Ask parents to write a short description of a time they observed their son/daughter acting in an understanding, caring, or empowering manner toward another person (e.g. friend, sibling, grandparent, neighbor, themselves, etc). Students or the teacher can read these in class or compile into a classroom reading available for any student.

## [All Grade Levels]

# Recognizing the Feelings of Others

<u>**Objective(s):**</u>

- Assist students in learning to recognize how others are feeling including the visual and auditory clues.
- Assist students to become more aware of how they express their own emotions.

<u>**Materials:**</u>

- Photos of people in various situations, doing different activities and expressing different emotions. (include pictures of people in various cultures and nations).
- Camera (digital)

<u>**Lesson Plan:**</u>

*Introduction:* Ask students why it might be important to be able to understand how others are feeling; give several examples such as asking someone to do something when they are tired, angry . . . etc. When is the best time to ask your mom for a favor or special privilege and how can you tell she is in a mood to more likely say, 'yes'? What are the clues you use to tell how someone feels? Then list on the board all the various emotions the students can identify in three minutes of brainstorming.

*Activity:* This activity is best when spread over several sessions. Have students look at the pictures of people around the world in various situations and try to identify how they think that person is feeling at the moment and why them might be feeling that way. There is no one, correct answer. Ask the students what clues they are focusing on that makes them think this is how the person is feeling.

Have students pantomime various feelings and have the rest of the class try to identify the emotion being demonstrated. Later have students make a sounds associated with each emotion. Acting in slow motion, have students use their whole bodies to show what it is like to feel happy, sad, angry, worried, proud, hurt, embarrassed, etc.

Take candid photos during the week of students in the class during various activities. Show the photos later in class and have classmates try to guess how the individual was feeling at that moment and possibly why.

***Closure:*** Have the students discuss how they felt doing these exercises on feelings. What did they learned from this activity and how could they use their new skills in identifying feelings in others to make their classroom a caring classroom.

## Suggested Classroom Follow-Up Activities:

- Use the feeling words as the week's spelling list or vocabulary list.

- Read students a popular piece of literature with frequent stops to discuss how they think the characters are feeling at the moment and why.

- Have students develop a manual about, "How to tell when someone is feeling . . . . and what to do about it". Students can write on a different emotion each day to develop their "User's Manual".

## Suggested Home Follow-Up Activities:

- Have students bring in pictures of their parents, siblings or other family members expressing various emotions.

- Have parents and students work together to assemble a collage of photos of people from magazines, newspapers, etc expressing various emotions and label each picture accordingly.

- Ask parents or another family member to write a short story about "A time when others did not understand how I felt". Ask them to include what that was like for them and what they wish others might have done if the were better at recognizing feelings in others. Read in class.

## *Empathy Skills*

### [All Grade Levels]

# My Scrapbook of Emotions

### Objectives:

- To help students become more aware of their emotions.
- To help students become aware of how different life situations affect their emotional responses.
- To become aware of how others feel under similar circumstances or have similar feelings under different circumstances.

### Materials:

- Three hole punched paper with words, "For me _____ is when _____ . . ."
- colored pencils or crayons
- 3 ring binders with dividers

### Lesson Plan:

*Introduction:*

Inform the students that today we are going to look at all the different emotions/feelings people experience in their daily lives. Ask, "How many of you have ever felt, happy? sad? worried? scared? bored? proud? etc., etc. So we have all experienced these feelings. But, how many of you would feel happy if your lunch today was egg salad? a fish sandwich? fruit and vegetables? How many would feel sad if this was your lunch? Suggest other such examples of how we each respond with different emotions to the same situation.

*Activity:* Have the students brainstorm all the emotions they can and list responses on the front board. Now hand out five sheets of paper to each student. Pick one emotion (best to begin with positive emotion such as happy, proud, etc). Instruct the students to fill in that emotion in the title (e.g. "For me HAPPINESS is when". Then have students draw a picture of their answer. Repeat for all five pages until each student has five pages identifying five situations in which they feel happy. [**Note**: repeat this activity daily or twice daily until five to ten emotions have been covered. Have students place their pages into their binder with each feeling in a separate divider section. Students will eventually each have a personal "Scrapbook of Emotions".

***Closure:*** Following each emotion have students share whichever responses they choose with classmates to learn more about what situations elicit similar and different emotional responses. Occasionally, invite students to take out their scrapbooks and identify if anyone's answers have changed since they made their scrapbook, e.g., no longer feels sad about tests, or scared to respond in class. Discuss the changeability of our emotions.

## Suggested Classroom Follow-Up Activities:

- *Reading*: During discussions of reading assignments invite students to identify the emotions each character is probably experiencing at that time and why.

- *History/Social Studies*: Have students identify situations or events when historical figures might have experienced each of the different emotions . . . organize as a room bulletin board or scrapbook.

- *Writing & Language Arts:* Invite students to write a short story about a fictional student and his "happiest, saddest, loneliest, scariest, etc., day in school". Have students read the stories and discuss how the character could have handled the situation differently or better; what could his/her classmates have done to help?

- *Music:* Have students identify the main feeling of singers in various songs. (e.g. wind beneath my wings, Tomorrow from Annie, Another Brick in the Wall, etc.)

## Suggested Home Follow-Up Activities:

- Have students interview a family member about, "A time when I felt . . . happiest, loneliest, most scared, etc." including how they handled the situation and/or wished they had handled it better. Share in class.

- Have students watch a tv show or movie at home with a parent or family member and identify specific scenes when the main character felt (happy, proud, worried, scared, loved, angry, fearful, timid, etc. ). Write these down for homework and share in class.

- Have students and their parents take photos of one another expressing various emotions . . . My Dad when he's happy, sad, angry, tired, etc; "My Mom when she is . . . ., etc., etc. Put into a "Scrapbook of Family Feelings" and bring to class.

[Grades 1-4]

# Pets and People Helping Each Other

**Objective(s):**

- To learn about how service dogs assist disabled people and why their jobs are so important.
- To promote an empathetic attitude toward people with disabilities.

**Materials:**

- *A Service Dog Goes To School*, by Elizabeth Simpson Smith
- List of vocabulary words (attached)
- http://www.ddfl.org/lessons3/helping.pdf

**Lesson Plan:**

*Introduction:* How do animals help people? Ask for specific examples. Define the words "disability" and "disabled." Why do some people with disabilities need help from animals? What if these people didn't have this type of help? When you see a person with a disability, how do you feel? How are they different than you? Explain that it is our differences that make us unique and special. What are some other things that make people unique? (i.e. skin color, hair color, race, religion, nationality, etc.). Ask them to pick a student in the class and make a list of five things that makes that student different from them; five things that make him/her the same as all of us?. What are some things that make animals different from each other? How do animals help us?

*Activities:* Read the book, A Service Dog Goes To School. Because of the length of this book (62 pages) it will take several days or weeks to read, depending upon your classroom schedule. After reading the book, ask the students to summarize it in written form, highlighting the main points and characters. If possible, invite a person with a disability, who has a working dog, to come to your classroom to speak to the students. It may be helpful to contact an organization that works with and trains dogs for this purpose, such as "Canine Companions for Independence," or "Freedom Service Dogs." Have the guest speaker discuss their experiences, their relationship with their dog and how their dog helps them to be independent and self-sufficient.

***Closure:*** Why are service dogs so important? How do they help people? Why is their training necessary? How can you help a disabled person feel comfortable when you approach them and their dog? What did you learn from the speaker? How has their service dog improved their life?

## Suggested Classroom/Academic Follow-Up Activities:

- Have the students write a letter to the guest speaker, telling her or him what they learned from the visit.

- Another good book about service animals is *Animals Helping With Special Needs*, by Clare Oliver, which explores a variety of different animals that help people with disabilities, including monkeys, dolphins, cats and horses.

- Have students investigate other ways animals have been used to help people in ways that benefit us all (locating lost people, rescue work, police work, cadaver dogs, drug dogs, etc).

## Suggested Home Follow-Up Activities:

- Have your students and their parent(s) make a list of how they care for their pet and how their pet enriches their lives as well.

- Provide parents with a list of animal rescue shelters, rehabilitation facilities or training centers for police, seeing-eye or companion dogs/pets. Encourage parents to take a "family field trip" to visit one of these facilities (or organize an evening or Saturday outing for parents/students to visit) and write a brief report about what they learned. Be sure to suggest that parents invite a classmate or two if they are unable to go with a parent.

**[Middle thru High School]**

# Empathy through Masks

**Objectives:**

- Students will increase their understanding of African culture
- look at the interconnectedness of scarcity and conflict
- examine some of the causes of ethnic conflict
- empathize with victims of ethnic conflict by gaining a more thorough understanding of its root causes

**Materials:**

- Paper Plates
- Assorted yarns (separated)
- Colored paper (separated)
- Markers, pencils, and crayons
- Decorative materials (separated)
- Scissors
- Glue

**Lesson Plan:**

*Introduction:* Divide the class into three groups: Group 1 has five students; and Groups 2 & 3 are equally divided with the remaining students. Write the word "SCARCITY" on the board. Explain to everyone that Groups 2 & 3 suffer from scarcity and see if they can come up with a definition for the word. Ask students what types of scarcity exist in under developed countries (e.g., scarcity of land, food, education, resources, etc.). Read the handout about the history of Rwanda.

*Activity:* Explain that each of the groups is going to create their own African masks but can only use the supplies handed out to their group. They cannot borrow supplies from other groups. Then provide Group 1 with samples from all of the materials available and tell them they can get more if they need them. Give Groups 2 & 3 only a limited quantity of certain supplies, and tell them they cannot get more if they run out. For example, Group 2 might only get yarn and crayons & Group 3 might get only colored paper and markers. Allow them to work on their masks. Hang them at the front of the room by their groups.

***Closure:*** Conduct a discussion on the appearances of the masks. Ask the groups about any problems that arose, how they felt about their resources and the other groups? Ask if they would have wanted additional supplies or different materials. Have the groups look at Group 1's masks. How do the students feel about their masks? Was the exercise fair to all of the groups? Did they feel jealous, resentful or other such feelings during the exercise?, Why? Label Group 1 "Europeans," Group 2 the "Tutsis" & Group 3 the "Hutus." Discuss how this scene is played out around the world.

## Suggested Classroom/Academic Follow-Up Activities:

• Explore the issues in Rwanda and how these led to the civil war and genocide in that country. Review the exercise and its implications if Group 1 were the European colonizers, Group 2 the Tutsis and Group 3 the Hutus. Europeans colonizers in Africa would either buy or take by force any supplies that they needed. The Hutus and Tutsis could not buy supplies so they could only take them through force. Have students discuss the problems each group would have to face (e.g., Europeans population small so resort to use of force as other groups seek to gain access to supplies. Suggest that Group 1 supports Group 3. If so, then what happens to Group 2? What happens when Group 1 returns to Europe? How do the two remaining groups feel and react? Combine Groups 1 & 2 into the Tutsi majority, but tell them that Group 3 still controls all the resources. How can Group 3 remain in charge? What can the Tutsis do? Have students research the issues and history of Rwanda focusing on their group's unique culture and interests; after discussions seek ideas on solutions to the Rwanda issue. Show the DVD, Hotel Rwanda.

• Have students investigate the issues in conflicts around the world that stem from limited access to resources (e.g., food, water, health care, education, housing, etc). Submit reports on their findings and recommendations for solving such world problems.

• Have students investigate issues in American or World history and the role limited resources have played in our internal conflicts and tensions (e.g. civil rights, women's rights, ADA legislation, suffrage movement, etc.)

## Suggested Home Follow-Up Activities:

• Ask parents to identify the "limited resources" within their family and discuss how they try to solve the problem (e.g. limited parental time for individual attention to each sibling, economic limitations for all the things each person desires, transportation, etc). Include a list of possible "family solutions".

• Have parents write a brief story of a time they felt cheated or discriminated against. Discuss how they felt and how they responded to the situation.

• Have parents discuss a time in their lives when they have personally witnessed injustice, discrimination or extreme poverty and hardship. How did they feel, react?

**[All Grade Levels]**

# Just For Laughs

**Objective(s):**

- Identify and practice effective communication skills and strategies
- To learn how to express empathy
- To learn to use self-control
- To learn how to help friends deal with bullying

**Materials:**

- Paper and pen

**Lesson Plans:**

*Introduction:* Introduce the students to this proverb: "People show their character by what they laugh at". Discuss its meaning.

Think of a T. V. show that makes you laugh . . . . The Simpsons, for example. Much of the humor in these shows is from the characters teasing or mocking each other. We think it is funny to laugh at these animated characters. Now ask students to think of a time when they have been made fun of or laughed at . . . . think of how that feels. Is this different from laughing at a T.V. show? In what ways?

Explore with the students the concept of "laughing at" vs. "laughing with". When we laugh at an embarrassing situation to deliberately mock or tease someone, we are being hurtful.

*Activity:* Group students into teams and have them choose a number from a bag . . . . #'s 1-6. Each of the six groups is instructed to come up with a scenario of laughing; odd number groups focus on examples of "laughing at" While even numbered groups focus on examples of laughing with another. Set appropriate ground rules for this activity (nothing directed at classmates, families, etc.). The groups will present their scenarios to the whole class and the class will discuss if the group was on target.

*Closure:* Revisit the proverb and ask the students to think about things they have laughed at today. How would they be judged? Remind that before we decide to mock or tease someone, we should ask ourselves how we'd feel if "in their shoes" . . . . just for laughs; just kidding!!

## Suggested Classroom/Academic Follow-Up Activities:

- Assign students the project of researching the history of humor and find examples of what we've found humorous over the centuries and the effects of humor politically and on our health and well being; include both positive and negative uses of humor.

- Research political humor (cartoons, jokes, satire, movies, internet, etc) and how it has been used over the course of history; e.g., colonial times, revolutionary war, political campaigns, etc.

- Have students bring in examples of current and past political cartoons and editorial satire and discuss what point(s) the author was trying to make.

## Suggested Home Follow-Up Activities:

- Have parents write about their favorite situation comedy from their childhood and why it was so funny to them. If possible, watch some videos or reruns of old comedies and films and discuss what people laughed at in those times.

- Have parents write a brief story about a time when they, or someone they know, was hurt by others "laughing at" instead of "laughing with" them.

- Ask parents to write a short story about a funny incident in their family that makes everyone laugh and feel closer as a family when retold . . . . Discuss in class why this kind of humor brings people closer rather than humor that is hurtful and moves people away from one another.

## [All Grade Levels]

# In Someone Else's Shoes

**Objective(s):**

- Identify and practice effective communication skills
- Learn strategies to express empathy.

**Materials:**

- Activity Sheet: "Five Steps in Someone Else's Shoes"
- Activity Sheet: "Someone Else's Shoes"

**Lesson Plan:**

*Introduction:* Write the saying, "Before you say anything about how someone is walking, walk a mile in his/her shoes" on the chalkboard. Form even numbered cooperative teams and direct the teams to brainstorm and write down a possible meaning of the saying. Ask each team to share their thoughts and discuss the teams' ideas. Explain that the statement is taken from an American Indian saying, "Before you judge or criticize someone, walk a mile in his/her moccasins." (Not an exact translation.). Then discuss the term "empathy", the ability to understand how another person might feel in a given situation. Explain that putting ourselves in another person's situation, and thinking about how we might feel in that situation, helps us to understand how that person might be feeling and thus respond in a helpful rather than harmful manner. Discuss how empathy builds opportunities for communication and effects relationships.

*Activity:* Distribute the Student Activity Sheet: "Five Steps in Someone Else's Shoes" and discuss each step. Present the situation on the "Someone Else's Shoes" activity sheet. Have students complete the sheet until they all have tic-tac-toe. Then, have students identify other situations they regularly encounter (e.g., first day at a new school and classroom) and could apply the Five Steps. Instruct the teams to brainstorm how they could use the "Five Steps" in that situation. Then have each team think of other situations where they might apply the "Five Steps". Ask each team to report out. After each team describes its situation and how its members decided to use the "Five Steps," lead the class in a discussion about what might happen if the "Five Steps" were not used and what individuals might say or do that is not helpful or even harmful.(what might some consequences be?).

***Closure:*** Lead the class in a discussion on how the "Five Steps" can be applied in everyday relationships and situations. How might the steps change how students get along with each other, their siblings, their teachers, their parents, and others? How might the "Five Steps" change the school and community?

## Suggested Classroom Follow-Up Activities:

- Discuss how characters are feeling in the books read for reading instruction or focus a book report on a particular situation in the book they are reading and how the character most likely felt and thought at that moment and how others responded in ways that demonstrated empathy or a lack of empathy.

- Have students find a current event in the newspaper, on the internet or in a magazine and write about what they think the individuals are feeling and thinking and how others might step in to show empathy and help them.

## Suggested Home Follow-Up Activities:

- Ask parents to write a brief paragraph about a time when they're son/daughter demonstrated caring and empathy toward a friend or family member.

- Have parents write a short story about a time when they stepped in to help someone who was experiencing a difficult time. Ask them to focus on how they could tell the person was feeling badly and what they did to help (say and do).

- Have students interview a family member, neighbor or family friend who lived through a difficult time or event in history (civil rights march, combat in a war, natural disaster, etc) and have them describe how they and others felt at the time and what others did that made it better or worse.

[Middle thru High School]

# The Civil War Up Close and Personal
## "Look Out My Window. What Do You See?"

**Objective(s):**

- Students will gain a deeper historical perspective through studying Huff's experience as portrayed in his drawings.
- Students will express empathy and historical knowledge through creating artwork
- Students will craft drawings and captions from the perspective of a Civil War identity.

**Materials:**

- Master copies of the "Drawings from Huff's Diary" and handouts are provided.
- "Drawings from Huff's Diary" (This lesson includes five drawings. Each small group will need one drawing; more than one group may use the same drawing.)
- "Analyzing Huff's Drawings" worksheet (one copy per group)
- Civil War character cards (one per student)
- Paper, pencils, colored pencils, markers, and/or crayons
- Needed materials can be found and printed from the website: http://chicagohistory.org/static_media/pdf/historylab/CHM-historylabTCWL4.pdf, http://chicagohistory.org/static_media/pdf/historylab/CHM-historylabTCWL3.pdf, and http://chicagohistory.org/static_media/pdf/historylab/CHM-historylabTCWL2.pdf

**Lesson Plan:**

*Introduction:* Copy the diary of William Huff from the website above and give to the students. Ask the class to imagine themselves in Huff's situation—far from their home, their family, and their friends. What people and things would they miss? How would they keep a record of their experiences while they were gone? Inform students that Huff kept a diary to record his experience through both words and pictures. Discussion questions include: What did Huff "see"? What do the drawings say about his state of mind and his feelings? What emotions are conveyed through Huff's artwork? By studying his artwork, do you have a more thorough and complete understanding of Huff and the life he lived? Why or why not?

*Activity:* Divide students into small groups and distribute one drawing from Huff's diary and a copy of the "Analyzing Huff's Drawings" worksheet to each group. Allow time for students to examine their drawing and complete the worksheet. Distribute a Civil War character card to each student. (If you have more students than characters, some students may receive duplicate characters; each student will still have a unique interpretation.) Once students have assumed their "identities," have them consider what their life was like during the war. Allow them time to review previous information, brainstorm ideas, and conduct research. In either case, instruct students to write a journal entry describing their life, feelings and thoughts at this time in the war. Have them also draw a picture of what he or she might see outside of his or her window in the 1860s as did William Huff. Remind students to include a caption with their drawings. The information in the drawing should relate to each student's character, match his or her diary entry (if applicable), and tell the viewer something about life during the Civil War.

*Closure:* Ask each group to present their drawing and journal entries to the class. After the presentations, hold a closing discussion to evaluate the drawings as a set. Sample discussion questions include: What did this student's character "see"? What do the drawings say about his/her state of mind and his feelings? What emotions are conveyed through the character's artwork? By studying the artwork, do you have a more thorough and complete understanding of this character and the life he/she lived? Why or why not? Have students present their drawings and captions to the class or exchange them with partners or in small groups.

## Suggested Classroom/Academic Follow-Up Activities:

- While students are drawing, you may want to play music from the Civil War to inspire you student writers & artists.

- Assign students to read more on life during the Civil war and discuss what they learned
    - Beatty, Patricia. *Charley Skedaddle.* New York: Troll, 2002.
    - — — —. *Jayhawker.* New York: Beach Tree, 1991.
    - Collier, James Lincoln and Christopher Collier. *With Every Drop of Blood.* New York: Delacourte Press, 1994.
    - Hunt, Irene. *Across Five Aprils.* New York, NY: Berkley Jam Books, 2002.
    - Murphy, Jim. *The Boy's War: Confederate and Union soldiers talk about the Civil War.* New York: Clarion Books, 1990.
    - Reeder, Carolyn. *Shades of Gray.* New York: Aladdin Paperbacks, 1999.
    - Fleischman, Paul. Bull Run (*Bull Run* offers a fictional look at the Civil War through the eyes of different characters.)
    - Examples of other Civil War diaries entries can be found at www.civilwarletters.com.

- Change the time, place, and view and have the students draw another picture from the new perspective, for example, an American prisoner in Vietnam.

## Suggested Home Follow-Up Activities:

- Ask parents and grandparents to write a "diary entry" describing their thoughts and feelings during a major world event (e.g., WWII, Korean War, Cuban Missile Crisis, Civil Rights marches, Vietnam War, Hurricane Katrina, 9/11, Fall of the Berlin Wall, etc. etc or any major world event important to the student's native country and family.

- Invite parents to read a book from a provided list with their son/daughter and to maintain a diary of their thoughts . . . both parent and child maintain a diary on what their thoughts, feelings are about the story and situation of the main character(s). Then discuss their diaries. Invite students to share diary entries of self and parents in class.
  ***Suggested Books:*** Diary of Anne Frank, A Long Way Gone, Your Name is Renee, etc.

# Civil War Character Profiles

**Name (s)**_____ **Date** _____

**PROFILE 1**
Male, 21 years old. You volunteered to become a Union soldier. Before the war you worked on your family farm in Iowa.

**PROFILE 2**
Male, 34 years old. You are originally from St. Louis, Missouri. You are a wounded Union soldier at a field hospital.

**PROFILE 3**
Female, 58 years old. You live in Chicago, Illinois. You have two sons both of whom are serving in the Union Army.

**PROFILE 4**
Male, 44 years old. You are a Union general from Pennsylvania. You have a wife and two children at home.

**PROFILE 5**
Female, 11 years old. You live in Massachusetts. Your father is serving in the Union army.

**PROFILE 6**
Male, 16 years old. You are from New York. Your father and brother are serving in the Union army. While they are gone, you are the man of the house.

**PROFILE 7**
Female, 26 years old. You live in Ohio. Your husband was killed in battle fighting for the Union.

**PROFILE 8**
Male, 26 years old. You are a Confederate soldier from Alabama but are currently being held in a Union prisoner-of-war camp.

**PROFILE 9**
Male, 21 years old. You serve in the Union army. You miss your fiancé who is waiting for you at home in New York.

**PROFILE 10**
Male, 26 years old. You are a slave from Mississippi and are working as a personal servant for your owner who is fighting in the Confederate army.

**PROFILE 11**
Male, 28 years old. You serve in the Confederate army. You miss your wife of five years. She is your childhood sweetheart and waits for you at home in North Carolina

**Profile 12**
Female, 20 years old. You are a slave who lives and works on a large Virginia plantation. Your owner is fighting for the Confederacy.

**PROFILE 13**
Male, 32 years old. You are from Pennsylvania and are a Union soldier held prisoner in a Confederate prison camp.

**PROFILE 14**
Male, 43 years old. You are originally from Louisiana. You work as a cook in a Confederate prison camp.

**PROFILE 15**
Female, 16 years old. You live in Mississippi. Your brother has just volunteered for the Confederate army.

**PROFILE 16**
Male, 19 years old. You work as a slave in Jefferson Davis's home in Mississippi.

**PROFILE 17**
Male, 51 years old. You are a general of the Confederate infantry.

**PROFILE 18**
Female, 28 years old. Your husband is in the Confederate army. While he is gone, you are running your family plantation in South Carolina.

**PROFILE 19**

Female, 22 years old. You are an African American living in the South. You are serving as a Union spy and working in the home of a Confederate general.

**PROFILE 20**

Male, 36 years old. You are a Union soldier from New Jersey living in a prison camp in the South.

[Middle – High School]

# The Bully

**Objective(s):**

- Students will learn to understand the various aspects of bullying and its effects
- Students will learn to identify role bystanders play in enabling bullying to occur
- Students will learn strategies for bullying prevention in their school and classroom
- Students will identify the commonality of feelings and concerns we all experience when moving and relocating

**Materials:**

- Purchase the text, The Bully, by Paul Langan (Bluford High Series #5).
- T-Charts entitled "The Many Faces of Bullying" (attached)

**Lesson Plan:**

*Introduction:* Ask students to share personal experiences they have had in relocating to a new school, community, country, etc. Ask questions such as, "Has anyone ever moved? If so, share what it was like; "What are the good things about moving? the problems?"

*Activity:* Introduce the book, The Bully, by asking what they believe the main problem will be for the title character, Darrell.

- Read Chapter #1 to the class
- Organize the class into groups of 3-4 students each and give each group a T-Chart
- Have 1/3 of groups mark their T-Chart, "Someone who is a Bully"; 1/3 of groups mark theirs "Someone who is Bullied" and the last 1/3 of groups mark theirs, 'Someone who is a Bystander"
- Have each group brainstorm a minimum of 5 descriptions for each column ("sounds like" and "looks like").

*Closure:* Have the groups share their ideas. Write each group's ideas on a chart and post for classroom display and reference.

## Suggested Classroom Follow-Up Activities:

- Have the students read the remaining chapters either individually, in pairs small groups, or as a class over the coming week or two (e.g. chapters 2-5, 6-8, 9-12).

- Have students reflect on what they have read by writing personal journal responses . . . invite to read aloud any parts of their entries they are willing to share and discuss with the class. Also, read and respond to their entries each day.

- Provide new T-Charts (attached) with story characters listed along the left column and three columns marked "Bully, Bullied and Bystander". Have small groups discuss examples of each student's role/experiences in bullying throughout the book

- Discuss how the characters could better handle each situation to stop/prevent bullying or being bullied.

- After completing the book, have students write a final journal entry describing what they have learned personally from this book and how it will impact their relationships in and out of school in the future.

## Suggested Home Follow-Up Activities:

- Invite parents to write a brief story of a time they were bullied or observed bullying behavior when they were children. How did they handle it then? How would they prefer to handle the same situation today if they could?

- Invite parents to use a T-Chart to brainstorm with their child ways to a) Handle situations when one is being bullied and b) Handle situations when one sees another student being bullied. Share in class and combine into a "Bully Prevention Strategies" classroom chart.

# T-Charts

## *Example 1:*
## The Many Faces of Bullying

Topic:     Bullies, Bullied or Bystanders

Sounds Like                                     Looks Like
(statements)                                      (behaviors)

## *Example 2:*
## Examples of Bullying in "The Bully"

| Character's Name: | Bullying | Bullied | Bystander |
| --- | --- | --- | --- |
| | | | |

## *Empathy Skills*
### [All Grade Levels]

# Readings in Life Lessons

**Objective(s):**

- Develop students' skills in identifying feelings, thoughts and motivations behind behavior.
- Develop skills in problem solving and handling their emotions.

**Materials:**

- Any book in which the character(s) are dealing with an issue common to all children of similar age to your students. (see your school librarian for assistance)

**Lesson Plan:**

### *Introduction:*

Inform students that today we will read a story that involves someone trying to deal with a common problem we all may face, or have dealt with, in our own lives. Listen carefully to see how well you can figure out how the character(s) are feeling, what they are thinking and why the act the way they do.

### *Activity:*

Read the story to the class or have the class read aloud together taking turns among volunteers. Have various students take the part of a given character and read their lines to make the activity more of a theatrical performance.

After reading the story, have students retell/recap the story in their own words stressing the various incidents, feelings and relationship dynamics as the story proceeded. Have the students problem into the changes in feelings and relationships or the behavior changes and why these behaviors, feelings and relationships changed.

Ask student to identify similar incidents from other stories or their own lives.

Invite students to explore the consequences of certain behavior; "what happened in a situation due to what behavior?"

What options did the characters have that might have led to a different outcome (good and bad).

*Closure:*

Ask students to arrive at a conclusion or generalization about the characters, how they felt/ thought, and the consequences of certain behavior choices. How can we apply this to our own lives??

## Suggested Classroom Follow-Up Activities:

- Provide a series of books for free reading in which characters are dealing with other issues common to children at this grade level. Have students summarize the stories and feelings, thoughts that motivated the various characters' behaviors and how this might be applied in their own lives.

- Brainstorm common problems amongst children of their age. Then have students write stories involving a character who is dealing with such a situation. Share stories or combine into a class Notebook for free reading time.

- Repeat the activity lesson during the coming weeks using stories with different issues.

## Suggested Home Follow-Up Activities:

- Have students interview a parent or other family member regarding incidents in their own childhood years when they dealt with a similar situation as the character in the book read in class. Have parents write a brief paragraph about the incident, how they felt, how they handled the situation and how they wished they had handled it.

- Ask parents to write a short story from their "family history" about a time when their parent/ grandparent/aunt-uncle, etc. felt hurt, proud, happy, scared, etc and what happened. Be sure that the story is from a time period before their child (your student) was born. Read and discuss stories in class.

- Provide your librarian develop a list of children's stories in which a character deals with a common childhood issue (e.g. bullying, making new friends, moving, feeling left out, moral decisions, loss of pet or loved one, illness, etc). Have students check out one of these books during library time and request parents to read the story with their child and discuss how the character felt, why behaved as he or she did and better options for handling such emotions and thoughts more effectively.

## [All Grade Levels]

# "In My Shoes"

### Objective(s):

- Develop students' ability to emphasize with someone different from themselves.
- Develop students' awareness and compassion for disabled individuals
- Develop students' awareness for how their actions help or hinder disabled people.

### Materials:

- Volunteer disabled adult speaker (blind, paraplegic, deaf, etc). If unable to arrange for a speaker, use a movie about a handicapped person.
- Blind folds, ear plugs, wheelchair

### Lesson Plan:

#### Introduction:

- Inform the students that today we are going to explore the life of people who face challenges from various disabilities. Introduce the guest speaker or show the movie.

#### Activity:

- Have him/her speak to the class regarding the disability and how he/she has learned to adapt and compensate.
- Allow time for students to ask open and honest questions following the presentation.
- After the presentation, have students take turns experiencing life as a disabled person. Students might be blindfolded and taken for a walk around the school/room, spend part of the day confined to a wheelchair, loose the use of an arm, wear earplugs, or in some way simulate the experience of being handicapped in some way.

#### Closure:

- End with a discussion focusing on the feelings they experienced when simulating the handicap.

## **Suggested Classroom Follow-Up Activities:**

- Repeat the various simulated handicap experiences so all students get a chance to experience each disability.

- Read a story or watch a movie regarding a disabled person and focus class discussion on how that person felt and what others did or didn't do that was helpful or hurtful.

- Have students write a thank you letter to the guest speaker focusing upon what they learned from the talk and what they most like about the speaker.

- Have students volunteer to provide tutoring or assistance to younger students receiving ESE services for various disabilities.

## **Suggested Home Follow-Up Activities:**

- Provide an opportunity for students and parents to volunteer or visit one day at the Special Olympics, local hospital or some other community program for disabled children or adults. Report on what they and parent learned.

- Provide parents with a list of movies involving a handicapped character and ask them to watch and discuss it with their son/daughter. Have parents include a brief paragraph regarding the movie and what they all learned and took from it.

- Ask parents to write a brief story about a disabled friend, colleague or family member and what that person had to do to compensate and/or how the parent assisted them.

[Grades Elementary thru High School]

# The Power of Empathy

**Objective(s):**

- To understand the suffering of others and foster a sense of empathy. The power of empathy will help students to ultimately understand what others feel and how they can help them.

**Materials:**

- Poster paper for chart

**Lesson Plan:**

*Introduction:* What is empathy? Why is it important to have empathy for others? Think of a person for which you have had empathy. What was this person's situation How were you able to assist this person once you listened to them and tried to understand how they were feeling? How has empathy helped you deal with your family and friends? What difficult challenges have you had in your life? How did you overcome them? Who helped you through them? How did they help you?

*Activity:* Students will think of a person that is facing a difficult challenge or who has overcome a hurdle in their life. Some examples: an AIDS patient; a recovering drug addict or alcoholic; a person who is, or used to be, homeless; a person with a disability; a victim of domestic violence. Students need to create interview questions and an interview format. They'll conduct the interview either in person or over the phone. The interview should serve to help each student understand the challenges, struggles, and victories of the person they're interviewing. The students should also try to understand how they and their community can help this person. Once the students have done their interviews, they need to write them in essay form, addressing all the issues mentioned. They'll each read theirs to the class. Afterwards, the class should work together on a chart of similarities that shows ultimately, how similar these challenges are. Invite several of the people interviewed to sit in on a panel discussion in the classroom. Prior to this, have the students think of questions they'll ask the panel. Focus on how it's possible to overcome hardships with the help and guidance of others.

***Closure:*** What's the most important thing you learned through your interview? How did empathy help you connect with these people and your community better? How can we work together to help people and animals that face hardships?

## Suggested Classroom/Academic Follow-Up Activities:

- Plan a field trip to visit an organization with which one of your interviewees is, or was, involved.

- Choose one person, group or agency to assist as a class project and develop a plan to "lend a helping hand" during the course of the school year.

## Suggested Home Follow-Up Activities:

- Ask parents to write a paragraph about a time they reached out to "lend a helping hand" to someone in need.

- Invite parents to assist in the class "helping hand project".

- Have parents write a short story about a time in their life when they needed a "helping hand" and who helped them (or what happened when they did not).

# Positive/Constructive
# Communication Skills

## [Grades 3 – 8]

# The Caring Tree

**Objective(s):**

- Develop student's skills in communicating caring and kindness in the classroom
- Increase student's awareness of how we communicate a sense of "belonging" to others in our class.
- Improve the classroom climate through communicating a sense of belonging and caring to all.

**Materials:**

- Flowers made from colored paper
- A tree trunk with branches made of construction paper and taped along one wall or bulletin board.

**Lesson Plan:**

*Introduction:* Begin the class by playing a downloaded copy of the theme song from the old TV series, Cheers. Ask students to listen carefully to the lyrics. Ask them to describe a time they went somewhere where "everyone knew your name and were always glad you came". Suggest that this is a goal of our classroom, to make it a place where we know everyone cares for us and is always glad we came.

*Activity:* Read the story of "Kyle" (attached). Have students brainstorm ways that they can reach out and show caring to people. Ask prompting questions to get them going such as, "what can you say or do to make a new student feel welcome", "what can you do to help someone who looks sad or left out?", "Think of a time when you lonely, hurt, discouraged, etc. . . what would you wish someone had done to help you feel better?"

When a student identifies an act of caring and kindness, write it on one of the paper flowers and hang the flower from the Caring Tree branches. Inform students that our goal is to make this tree bloom as we develop our Caring Classroom.

*Closure:* Play the Cheers theme song one more time. Inform students that for the next week we will explore ways to express caring and kindness to others. They should look this week for acts of caring and kindness from friends, family, teachers, etc and share these in class so we can add additional flowers to make this tree bloom brighter.

## Suggested Classroom Follow-Up Activities:

- Each day take a few minutes for students to share ways that they have been kind or helpful to a friend, family member, neighbor, classmate or stranger or ways others have shown caring and kindness to them. Write each new example on a flower and post it on the Caring Tree.

- Have students identify a teacher or family member who has demonstrated an act of caring and kindness to them and write a thank you letter to that person and deliver it to them.

- Introduce stories in class involving acts of caring and kindness to others (see librarian for suggestions)

- Have students work in small groups to develop a vocabulary list of "Words of Caring and Kindness". List all the words one might use to express thoughtfulness, caring and kindness to another.

- Have students look through newspapers and magazines to find stories of people who demonstrated an act of caring and kindness. Share these news stories in class.

## Suggested Home Follow-Up Activities:

- Have students with their parents develop a collection of photos (from family albums or take photos themselves) of people in their family who have been caring and kind. Create a "Caring Family Gallery" by posting the photos on a sheet of poster board with a caption for each as to what act of caring and kindness each person has demonstrated.

- Ask parents to write a short description of "A Time Someone was Especially Caring and Kind in My Life" or, "The Most Caring Person in my Life". Share these stories in class.

- Have parents work with their child to develop a list of "Ways we show caring in our family without speaking". This is a list of "acts of kindness" rather than words of kindness.

# Theme Song from
## *"CHEERS"*

_____

Making your way in the world today takes everything you've got.
Taking a break from all your worries sure would help a lot.
Wouldn't you like to get away?
Sometimes you want to go
Where everybody knows your name,
And their always glad you came

You want to be where you can see
Our troubles are all the same.
You want to be where everybody knows your name.

You want to go where people know,
People are all the same.
You want to go where everybody knows your name.

# *Story of Kyle*

One day when I was a freshman in high school, I saw a kid from my class walking home from school. His name was Kyle. It looked like he was carrying all of his books home for the weekend. I remember thinking to myself, "Why in the world would anyone bring home all his books on a Friday? He must really be a nerd". I had quite a weekend planned a party that night and then a pickup football game with my friends Saturday morning. So, I shrugged my shoulders and went on.

As I was walking a bit further, I saw a bunch of kids running toward hi. They ran at him, knocked all his books out of his arms and tripped him so that he landed in the dirt; then walked off laughing with while taunting him with the comments, "Geek, Nerd"! His glasses went flying and I saw them land in the grass about ten feet away. As he looked up, I saw this terrible sadness and hopelessness in his eyes. My heart went out to him. So, I jogged over to him and as he crawled around looking for his glasses, I could see a tear in his eye.

As I handed him his glasses, I said, "Those guys are just a bunch of jerks. They really should get lives!" He looked at me and said, "Hey thanks!" There was a big smile on his face; one of those smiles that shows genuine gratitude. I helped him pick up his books and asked him where he lived. As it turned out, he lived near me so I asked him why I had never seen him before. He said he'd gone to a private school before now and had just transferred to the public high school this fall to save his parents the high expense of tuition. Private school kids and public high school kids didn't really hang out much with each other in our town. We talked all the way home and I helped him carry some of his books. He turned out to be a pretty neat kid so I asked him if he would like to play football on Saturday with me and my friends. He said, Yes.

We hung out together all weekend and the more I got to know Kyle, the more I liked him. And my friends all thought the same. Monday morning came, and there was Kyle with that huge stack of books again. I stopped him and said, "Dang boy, you are gonna really build some serious muscle with this pile of books everyday!" He just laughed and handed me half the books.

Over the next four years, Kyle and I became best friends. When we were seniors, we began applying to colleges. Kyle decided to go to Georgetown University and I went to our state university. I knew that we would always be close friends and that the miles would never be a problem. Kyle was going to study pre-med and go on to medical school I had a football scholarship and planned to get a degree in business. Kyle was named valedictorian of our graduating class. I would tease him all the time about being such a book nerd. As valedictorian, Kyle had to prepare a speech for graduation, I was just glad it wasn't me having to get up there and speak.

On graduation day, I saw Kyle. He looked great. He was one of those guys that really found himself during high school. He filled out and actually looked good in glasses. He even seemed to have more dates than me and all the girls loved him! Sometimes, I must admit I felt a bit jealous. And today was one of those days. I could see that he was really nervous about his speech. So, I smacked him on the back and said, "Hey, big guy don't worry, you'll do great!" he looked at me with one of those looks (the really grateful kind like on that first day we met) and just smiled. "Thanks", he said.

As he started his speech, Kyle cleared his throat and began, "Graduation is a time to thank those who helped you make it through those tough years. Your parents, your teachers, your brothers and sisters, maybe a coach or neighbor but, mostly your friends! I am here to tell all of you that being a friend to someone is the best gift you can give them. I am going to tell you a story." I just looked at my friend with disbelief as he told the story of the first day we met. He had been planning to kill himself over the weekend. He talked of how he had cleaned out his locker so that his Mom wouldn't have to do it later and that was why he was carrying all his stuff home. He looked right at me and gave me a little smile. "Thankfully, I was saved. My friend saved me from doing the unthinkable".

I heard the gasp go through the crowd as this handsome, popular boy told us all about his weakest moment when the teasing, bullying and loneliness seemed just too much bear. I saw his mom and dad looking at me and smiling that same grateful smile. Not until that very moment did I realize its depth.

———————————————————————

*Never underestimate the power of your actions! With one small gesture you can change a person's life, for better or for worse through what we choose to do, or not to do. Sometimes we just don't stop to think about how we are impacting those around us or recognize what incredible potential we each have within us to make this a better place for ourselves and for others.*

## Positive/Constructive Communication Skills

### [All Grade Levels]

# Listening Designs

**Objective(s):**

- Increase students' attending skills
- Increase students' ability to express themselves clearly and precisely to others
- Increase students' awareness of how easily miscommunication takes place in our daily lives.

**Materials:**

- Prepare a series of envelopes each filled with various shapes cut from colored construction paper. Include large and small circles, triangles, squares, octagons, rectangles, etc of all colors). Each envelope should consist of the identical set of colored shapes of various sizes.

**Lesson Plan:**

*Introduction:* Ask students how many think they communicate clearly to others. Then ask how many have ever felt misunderstood by someone. How is it that so many good communicators are so often misunderstood? Let's try an experiment in communicating clearly.

*Activity:* Students are paired with a partner for the activity. Sitting back to back, one is designated as the communication "sender" and the other as the communication "receiver" Each student is given one of the identical envelopes of colored shapes. The 'sender" begins by using his/her shapes to create a design on the floor in front of him/her. As s/he does so, s/he tells the "receiver" how to make the identical design. The receiver must attempt to make an identical design on the floor in front of him/her. However, the "receiver" is NOT allowed to speak (i.e. no questions, clarification requests, etc).

After a few minutes, have the students stop and compare their designs. Discuss what went wrong. Was miscommunication a problem? How can they solve the problem? Then have them try again and see if they can improve their communication. Reverse roles so each student has the chance to be "sender" and "receiver".

Retry the activity but this time, allow receivers to ask clarifying questions of the sender to make sure he/she correctly understands how to proceed with the design.

***Closure:*** Follow the standard closure questions regarding: "What happened?, "How did they feel at each step?", "When have they encountered a situation in their own lives when they misunderstood or where misunderstood? "How can we use this information to better handle such situations in the future?"

## Suggested Classroom Follow-Up Activities:

- During class discussions, have students begin by repeating what the previous speaker said and asking if he/she correctly understood. Then they can give their own opinion, idea, etc.

- Have students review current events in the newspaper for examples of people being misunderstood or miscommunication of their ideas. Include examples of deliberate misleading communication in advertising, politics, etc.

- Have students stop and ask questions during math, science etc classes which seek clarification to be sure they fully understand directions, lessons, etc. Make it normal and acceptable to ask clarifying questions during class lessons.

## Suggested Home Follow-Up Activities:

- Have students interview their parents or other family members about a time they felt misunderstood by others. How did they handle it? What could they have done to make the situation work out better?

- Ask parents to watch TV commercials and infomercials to identify examples of foggy, obtuse communication that can lead to the public misunderstanding (e.g. disclaimers quickly stated after dramatic benefits suggested in ads for medications, diets, etc).

- Have parents and students write a brief story together about a time when they experienced miscommunication with one another, what happened and how they could handle this better in the future.

## *Positive/Constructive Communication Skills*

### [All Grade Levels]

# Encouragement Booklets

**Objective(s):**

- To develop a positive classroom climate
- To make students aware of the impact of both Negative/Destructive and Positive/Constructive Comments.
- To make students aware of how their communication is perceived by others and how that reflects upon other's opinions of you.
- To help students feel safe, valued, and connected (belonging) in the classroom.

**Materials:**

- Story of Mark (attached)
- Paper(s) with the names of each student listed and space for student's comments next to each person's name.

**Lesson Plan:**

*Introduction:* Ask students, "Have you ever heard someone say something critical or hurtful about you?" How did you feel about yourself, the person who said it?" This is called Negative/Destructive Communication. Then, ask "Has anyone ever said something positive or encouraging to you? what did they say? how did you feel about yourself? about the person who made the comment?. This is called Positive/Constructive Communication. Note that both types have very powerful affects on others and say a lot about the type of person we are ourselves. Tell the students you are going to read a story to them about the power of positive/constructive communication. Then read the story of Mark (attached to this lesson).

*Activity:* Provide each student with a paper that has the name of each student in the class listed along the left column and then sufficient space for writing their comments about each person. This will likely require 2 sheets of paper double-sided. Have students spend a few minutes writing something positive about each and every classmate; something they admire, like, appreciate or enjoy about that particular person. i.e., "I like it when you . . ." ; I appreciate it when you . . . "I like the way you . . ."

When done, collect the papers and type up a sheet for each student listing all the positive comments the classmates wrote about him/her (good task for a teacher aide or parent volunteer). Edit out any negative/destructive comments. When completed, give each student his or her Encouragement Comments.

***Closure:*** After handing out the list of positive/constructive comments to each student, ask how They felt when they started this activity. How did it feel to express positive/encouraging Comments to others? How did you feel just before you got your comments sheet? How did you feel after reading them? How does hearing such comments from classmates affect our class as a group? How can we do this in our day to day lives in the classroom and outside?

## Suggested Classroom Follow-Up Activities:

- Make a classroom bulletin board entitled "Positive/Constructive Communication". Have students identify comments they heard that day from classmates or staff that were Positive/ Constructive. Type up the comments (in quotes) and put on the bulletin board as examples. Do this activity daily for the week.

- Put famous quotes about positive communication around the room. Have student do internet searches on quotes about encouragement and positive communication to add to the classroom.
  e.g. *"Keep away from people who try to belittle your ambitions, small people always do that, but the really great make you feel that you too, can become great"* **Mark Twain**
  *"The best way to cheer yourself, is to try to cheer someone else up".* **Mark Twain**
  *"When you cannot get a compliment any other way, pay yourself one!"* **Mark Twain**

## Suggested Home Follow-Up Activities:

- Have students write Positive/Constructive comments about each parent and/or sibling as they did with classmates to bring home and present to their family members. (e.g. "Things I like about my Mom/ Dad/Sister/Brother/Grandma etc")

- Have parents write a Letter of Encouragement identifying things they admire, like, appreciate or enjoy about their child (see attached example format . . . )

- The teacher can also write a similar "Note of Encouragement" about each student to read to each student and then mail to the parents. (see attached example).

**<u>Format Examples:</u>**

# Letter of Encouragement
### (parent to child)

Dear _____,

    In the course of our busy day-to-day lives, I sometimes forget to let you know all the things you do that make me so proud and happy to have you as my _____. So I thought I'd take this moment to let you know some of the special things I enjoy about you and our relationship.

_____

# Letter of Encouragement
### (child to parent)

Date:

Dear _____,

    In the course of our busy day-to-day lives, I sometimes forget to let you know all the things you do that make me so proud and happy to have you as my Mom/Dad/Grandparent. So I thought I'd take this moment to let you know some of the special things I enjoy about you and our relationship.

## Positive/Constructive Communication Skills

### [All Grade Levels]

# Round Robin Story Telling

**Objective(s):**

- Develop students listening skills
- Assist students in learning to listen to one another and build off other's ideas
- Develop cooperative learning environment

**Materials:**

- String or twine cut into pieces approximately 6 feet long
- audio tape recorder

**Lesson Plan:**

*Introduction:* Inform the class that today we are going to practice how to link ideas so as to develop something by all of us that none could have done alone.

*Activity:* Select a group of about six students to sit in a circle at the front of the room with the teacher. Each child is handed the end of one piece of string. The teacher holds the other end of all the strings. Instruct students that when the teacher pulls on their string, they are to begin adding to the creative story being told; when the string is pulled a second time they stop and another child's string will be pulled so he/she can add to what was said so far. Stress that it is important to listen closely to one another so that they will understand what direction the story is taking and can add to it.

Begin the story with no more than two lines, e.g., "Once there was a young girl who had just moved to a new town. On her first day at her new school, . . ." now pull a child's string to finish this sentence and add one or two more, and then randomly move around the circle having different children add to the story until they have a finished group story.

Tape record the story and have a parent volunteer type it up and build a classroom binder with their Round Robin Stories.

*Closure:* Ask students how it felt to do this activity. Did they have any difficulty making the connection between the previous ideas and the new one they wanted to add? How is this skill important when you work with others?

## Suggested Classroom Follow-Up Activities:

• Continue the activity with at least two groups daily until all have participated at least once.

• During any class discussions, use the same approach where each student must respond to what the previous person said rather than to the teacher's original question.

• Have students engage in creative writing activities in small groups (4-5 each). Each student begins to write a story and then after a few minutes the teacher instructs each person to pass their paper on to the person on their right and add to their story. Continue until all have added a portion to each group member's creative story.

## Suggested Home Follow-Up Activities:

• Have students write the first paragraph for a creative story. Then have them bring this home for homework and ask each family member to write 3-4 lines each. Have each person put their initials beside their portion of the story until they've developed a "Family round robin story". Invite students to share these stories in class.

• Ask parents to begin a story (one paragraph) about a special or fun time in their family. Then have the students complete the story or have each family member add another section about that event.

## *Positive/Constructive Communication Skills*

### [All Grade Levels]

# Responding to the Previous Speaker

## Objective(s):

- Develop students listening skills
- Improve communication patterns in the classroom moving from a "Wheel" Communication patterns with teacher at the hub and spokes to each student to a more functional "Switchboard" pattern where every student communicates directly with one another.

## Materials:

- A current event or article from a newspaper or magazine

## Lesson Plan:

*Introduction:* Arrange the class in one large circle. Tell students that we are going to discuss a current event or issue (world, local, or school focused) but each student must can only contribute by first responding in some way to what the previous speaker said. Require students to look directly at the last contributor as they link their comments to what has previously been said. Then they can add another comment.

*Activity:* Read an article or raise an issue currently impacting their lives. Then ask a related question such as, "What do you feel is the problem or the solution to this issue . . . ?". To help them get started, call on one student to give some views on the question. Then ask for a volunteer to respond to the first student. Continue until every group member has had at least one chance to reply to another's remarks and add their own views, ideas, etc.

*Closure:* Follow the normal closure discussion format focusing on what happened, how they felt at first, later on and how this skill could be applied in their daily lives.

## Suggested Classroom Follow-Up Activities:

- Have "all class" discussions on various topics in science, social studies or literature proceed using the same format.

- Read or play (video or audio) a speech, story or poem, by a known writer or politician, and then have students respond as if speaking to that author or speaker.

## Suggested Home Follow-Up Activities:

- Have students interview their parents or family members regarding a specific issue or topic from class. Have students then present their parent's views and their written response/thoughts to what the parent said.

- Invite parents to hold a family discussion at the dinner table using the "Responding to Previous Speaker" format. Write then a brief description of what they observed happening in the family communication.

# *Positive/Constructive Communication Skills*

## [Elementary & Middle School]

# **<u>Mirroring</u>**

<u>**Objective(s):**</u>

- Develop students' attending skills
- Develop students' awareness of non-verbal communication

<u>**Materials:**</u>

- none needed

<u>**Lesson Plan:**</u>

*Introduction:* Write on the board phrases such as: "By their actions you will know them", "Don't listen to their lips, but rather, watch their fists and feet", "Walk the talk" and "Listen with your eyes". Have students what these common sayings mean. After concluding that it is important to pay attention to people's actions and not just their words, ask, "How many here think they are good observers of people? Today we will see just how good you are.

*Activity:* Begin by pairing students with a partner and have them sit on the floor or in chairs facing one another. One student in each pair is designated as the "mirror" and the other as the "person" in front of the mirror. [Note: with younger students briefly discuss the fact that mirrors are stationary so you cannot move from being directly in front of the mirror]. Have the "person" in each pair move in SLOW MOTION using hand and feet movements, facial expressions, etc. The "mirror" partner must follow and mirror each and every movement, expression, etc. After several minutes, have the partners reverse roles.

With older students, or if your class/group is doing exceptionally well, challenge them to see if they can do this at the "advanced level". In this situation, both partners are simultaneously a "mirror" and the "person" (leader and follower). Here, either person my initiate a movement and the other must follow requiring total attending to one another and moving as one. You may also try having students repeat the exercise while standing up (i.e. the full-length mirror).

*Closure:* Close the session by using the standard closure questions for this program. What happened? How did they feel as they did the activity?", Have you ever experienced a problem situation in your life when you didn't pay attention or weren't attended to? How can we use what we've learned in our own lives?

## Suggested Classroom Follow-Up Activities:

- During reading assignments, have students demonstrate the body language they would expect to see in the various characters at different points in the story.

- Discuss current world events or historical events and have students demonstrate how they feel people would look that expressed their feelings about that event.

- Show pictures of people at various times in history and have students identify how their body language tells us about how they felt at that moment in time (e.g. holocaust prisoners, V Day celebrations, inauguration of President Obama, graduation ceremony, etc)

## Suggested Home Follow-Up Activities:

- Ask parents to write down a list with their student of ways members of their family express how they are feeling without using words (e.g. folded arms and stern look, smiling, rolling eyes, etc). Identify each family member's favorite non-verbal expression.

- Have parents and their child mutually complete a questionnaire re: "I know when my mother/ father/son/daughter is (upset, hurt, worried, happy, proud, excited, confused, discouraged, etc) when . . . .". Or, "I know it's a good (bad) time to ask for a favor/help when my parent . . . ." Invite them to talk about how they watch one another for non-verbal communication as to what they are thinking and feeling.

- Have parents develop a "family scrapbook" with photos showing family members at various times and write below each what the individuals in each photo were "saying" with their body language.

# Giving and Receiving Appreciations

## Objective(s):

- Students learn to appreciate fellow classmates
- Students learn that their good actions and character is recognized and appreciated by fellow classmates

## Materials:

- 3 small sheets of paper
- Pen or pencil

## Lesson Plan:

*Introduction:* Teacher will have a discussion with students about the meaning of "appreciation". They will also have a discussion about how it feels to do something nice for someone and not get any recognition or appreciation. Focus on specific examples!

*Activity:* Teacher will then assign each student 3 classmates to write about. Students will use one piece of paper for each classmate and write 3 things that they appreciate about them. Encourage students to be as specific as possible. The students will then turn in their papers to the teacher (for review) and the teacher will then combine the appreciation comments about each student into a single page. All comments are then placed in a single binder entitled, "Appreciating our Classmates". Leave the binder in some designated area for students to review as they please.

*Closure:* At the end of the day or learning block, have children read their comments to themselves and talk about what it felt like to realize that they are appreciated. Then talk about how you make other people feel when you let them know that you appreciate them.

## Suggested Classroom/Academic Follow-Up Activities:

- Have students write "Letters of Appreciation" to people in their school who contribute their life at school (e.g., custodian, cafeteria workers, administrators, art/music/PE teachers, etc.

- Have students identify someone who makes an important contribution to our lives in the community and write a "Letter of Appreciation" to that individual (e.g., police, fire dept, coach/instructor, mailman, waste collection service, or other community services workers.

- Have students research famous individuals in history who have made a contribution to improving our lives. Have them write an essay expressing appreciation for what this person contributed to our lives.

## Suggested Home Follow-Up Activities:

- Have students write "Letters of Appreciation" to their parents, grandparents and/or sibling.

- Ask parents to write a "Letter of Appreciation" to their son/daughter and send it to school after sharing with their child

- Ask parents to write about someone in their lives who they particularly appreciate and why.

# Cooperation Skills

# Cooperation Skills

## [All Grade Levels]

# Five Squares Puzzle

## Objective(s):

- Develop student's cooperation skills
- Develop student's problem solving skills
- Identify student response style to challenging tasks

## Materials:

- Five squares puzzle pieces in identical envelopes (see attached diagram)
- Tables or desks organized together with five chairs facing one another.

## Lesson Plan:

*Introduction:* Have students describe a time they had to solve a problem or accomplish a difficult task as part of a team effort. Inform students that "team problem solving skills" are amongst the most important skills needed in the workplace. Today, we will practice our team problem solving skills.

*Activity:* Place students in groups of five around tables and give each student in the group an envelope containing three puzzle pieces (see directions attached). Inform them that their task is to form five squares of equal size from these puzzle pieces. The group is not finished until each member has in front of him/her a perfect square of the same size as that in front of each of the other members of the group.

## RULES:
- No member may speak.
- No member may ask another for a card or in any way signal to another person to give him/her a card.
- No member may take a card from another member.
- No member may assemble a square for another member.
- There is no time limit.
- Members MAY give cards to other members of the group but not indicate how it is to be used.
- Pieces MAY be given to another player but cannot be placed in the center for anyone to take.

107

***Closure:*** Follow the group follow up discussion questions for the Resiliency skills program. Have students identify how they felt at the beginning, middle and end of the activity. What did others do that was helpful versus frustrating or problematic for the group?. Finally, ask students to think of situations where such cooperation is needed for all to be successful.

## Suggested Classroom Follow-Up Activities:

- Have your students complete similar "five square puzzles" using pieces that combine into complete sentences (English) or correct mathematical equations (mathematics).

- Introduce "cooperative learning" activities in which the team's goal is for all members to obtain a mastery score on the final exam.

- **NOTE:** the teacher should observe how the various students respond at the beginning of the activity. Their responses can be very insightful in regard to how they respond to challenging learning activities (e.g. some withdraw and give up, some seek assistance immediately due to self-doubt, some focus on telling others what to do and do not exam own behavior, some try to take charge, some refuse to participate in a passive aggressive manner, others become very competitive and seek to be first and then withdraw even if their puzzle is done incorrectly, etc)

## Suggested Home Follow-Up Activities:

- Have students make their own puzzles using language or math puzzles and see how their family handles the task.

- Ask parents to share (e.g., write a short note) with their child how "group cooperation and problem solving occurs in their work place. Discuss in class.

- Have parents and students make a list of examples of group problem solving in sports, business, and various professions.

-

# *Five Squares Format:*

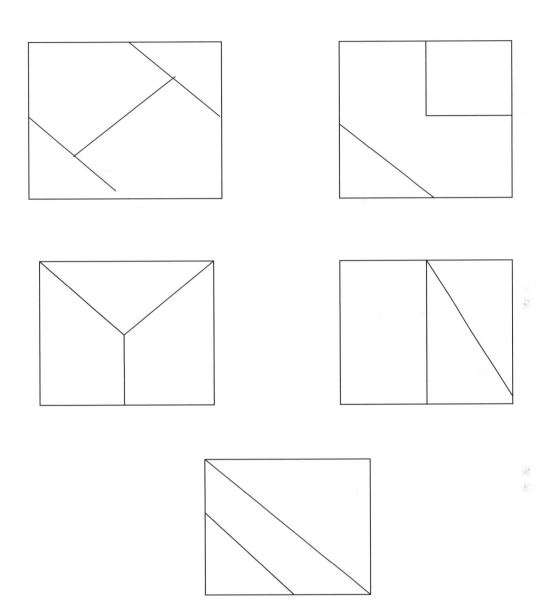

## DIRECTIONS

For each design, use a 6-inch square piece of heavy paper. Mark the squares as above. Then, randomly mark each puzzle piece as either A, B, C, D, or E. Cut out the puzzle pieces and place all A pieces in the "A" envelope, B pieces in the "B" envelope, etc. Place students in groups of 5 facing one another at a table and give each student one of the five envelopes. Then, follow the instructions as on the previous page

# Group Sit

**Objective(s):**

- Develop students' cooperation skills
- Develop a classroom climate focused on cooperation and success by all rather than competition.
- Help students learn how their actions impact success or failure of others and the group.

**Materials:**

- none needed

**Lesson Plan:**

*Introduction:* Ask the class how many have ever played a team sport. How do teammates have to cooperate together if their team is to be "competitive", i.e. able to win? Write the equation

$X = Y2 - Y/2$ on the board. Explain that this tells us how many cooperative pairs exist in any team or group effort. For example, a soccer team has 11 players so $(112 - 11) = 110$ and divided by 2 = 55 cooperative pairs on the field at any one time. Tell students that today we are going to practice how to make our class function like a "Winning team".

*Activity:* Put students in groups of about 10 students per group all standing in a circle. Tell students to turn to their right. Our goal is for everyone to sit in the lap of the person behind them until the whole group is sitting, without chairs, and hands/arms extended over our heads. Remind them this means you must be careful to work as ONE, and to make sure you create a lap space for the person in front of you while sitting down yourself. Then, have the student put their hands on the waist of the person in front of them. Now take sideways step toward middle of the circle. Continue until each group is closely packed so the task is possible.

Have each group go half way down (do not sit yet) and make sure they have a Lap behind them to sit on. When ready, instruct the groups to slowly go down and sit on lap of person behind you. When all seated, raise hands above heads to show they are sitting in a group without chairs.

If a group falls (domino style), have a brief discussion regarding what went wrong and how to correct the problem, then try again. Stress that the whole group succeeds or nobody succeeds in a cooperation game.

Once all are successful, challenge them to go for a "class record" with more students per group until eventually the whole class can do this together in one big circle.

***Closure:*** Discuss using the standard format. Discuss how this is important in our Cooperative learning groups and how we can use these skills in class to make sure everyone in our class is successful mastering every subject.

## Suggested Classroom Follow-Up Activities:

- Engage in classroom cooperative learning activities

- Use a "J-curve" cooperative learning test format. Have students take an exam on Monday for a lesson/skill/chapter they will be covering in the coming weeks and count the total number of correct responses for the class combined. Graph on a wall chart with vertical line = total correct answers in class and horizontal = day of the week. Retest each day with the class goal of trying to achieve a classroom PR (performance record) i.e. largest total number of correct responses to date . . . . the curve should eventually follow a J-curve profile.

- Challenge the class to see if they can teach this to other students at school and go for a school record.

## Suggested Home Follow-Up Activities:

- Have students teach the game to their family and see if they can do it successfully.

- Have students and parents list all the ways they must cooperate at home for their family to function well. Include ideas on how to improve cooperation at home.

- Have parents write a brief story about times when they have to work cooperatively at work and what problems sometimes occur with their "teamwork" in the job.

# Group Stand

## Objective(s):

- Develop students' cooperation skills
- Develop a classroom climate focused on cooperation and success by all rather than competition.
- Help students learn how their actions impact success or failure of others and the group.

## Materials:

- none needed

## Lesson Plan:

*Introduction:* Inform students that we are going to try a new cooperative game and challenge ourselves to set a classroom record.

*Activity:* Pair students off and have them sit back-to-back on the floor. Have students lock elbows with their partner and pull their feet up as close as possible with both feet remaining flat on the floor. Inform students that the objective is for each pair to stand up without letting go of the elbow lock and without moving their feet.

Conduct a brief discussion as to how they managed to solve the problem and the mistakes they made in finding the solution. Then challenge them to do this with larger groups. Begin with 4 per group ( 2X2 with backs together with partner, lock one elbow with person sitting next to you and one with person behind you.) and have them do a group stand. Then increase to 6, 8, 10 etc until eventually the entire class can sit in two rows, back-to-back and do a Group Stand.

*Closure:* Discuss how they learned to solve the problem and what can cause the whole group to succeed or fail in achieving their goal. Discuss how they can use this group cooperation in class? Challenge the class to recruit friends and other students to set increasingly larger records for the group stand.

## Suggested Classroom Follow-Up Activities:

- Ask the Physical Education teacher to initiate some cooperative games in P.E. such as cooperative volleyball (keep the ball up), parachute toss, etc.

- Have students engage in cooperative learning activities requiring the whole group to master a skill or knowledge set (e.g. a science or math exam in which each group member receives 90% or better correct) to be successful.

## Suggested Home Follow-Up Activities:

- Have students attempt to get their families involved in the Group Stand at home

- Have parents discuss with their child how cooperation and team work is needed at their job and then have students discuss this in class.

## Cooperation Skills

[All Grade Levels]

# All Aboard the Lifeboat

**Objective(s):**

- Develop students' cooperation skills
- Prepare students for cooperative learning activities in class
- Teach group problem solving skills

**Materials:**

- A board or gym matt (2" or more thick and approximately 4'X 2')

**Lesson Plan:**

*Introduction:* Inform students that today we are going to play a game to test their ability to work as a team and cooperate so everyone succeeds. Discuss briefly the importance of group cooperation in daily tasks (e.g., sports, the school staff, classmates, world of work, animals, etc).

*Activity:* Place the mat or board in the middle of an open floor space. Ask students to imagine that our classroom is a ship and it is slowly sinking. The board/mat is our only life raft and we must try to get everyone on board so all survive; and the water (floor) is shark infested so nobody can have a foot or body part touching the floor. We'll have to be creative to fit everyone on board until the rescue helicopters and ships arrive. Then, one by one call on each student in the class to "get on board" the life raft. Those already on board will need to find ways to add each new person. Try several times to see how many they can get on board. If they succeed with the entire class, challenge them again with a slightly smaller "life boat".

*Closure:* Follow the Developing Resilient Youth's Concluding Discussion format. Discuss the importance of group cooperation in the school and in our classroom, have students give specific examples of cooperation in the classroom; Why do some people have trouble cooperating?; How can we help them become better at cooperation?

## Suggested Classroom Follow-Up Activities:

- Establish an "eye spy" bulletin board in the room and daily add notes identifying examples of cooperation which the teacher caught the day before. Aim to include at least one example of cooperative behavior by each student before the week is done.

- In science class, discuss how animals survive by cooperating. Then assign the students to groups of four. Give each person in each group one of four animals to research as to how it survives through cooperative behaviors (e.g. deer, lions, ants, bees, frogs, birds, gazelles, elephants, etc). Students will then be sent off with those other students researching the same animal and provided library/computer time to research their animal and identify ways the animal uses cooperation for all to survive. Each person will then prepare a written and illustrated report to present to the class and their group. After the presentations, give an exam (see below) in which the students must identify three things about each animal's form of cooperation. After grading the exams, let the students discuss the questions. Let them know that this afternoon, or tomorrow morning, they will retake the exam but the goal is to get everyone in your group with a score of 100%. Repeat until all successful.

## SAMPLE:
## Animals Cooperating for Survival
## Worksheet

1.  List three things you learned about cooperation among deer.

    _____
    _____
    _____

2.  List three things you learned about cooperative behavior among elephants.

    _____
    _____
    _____

## Suggested Home Follow-Up Activities:

- Ask children to interview a parent or family member about how cooperation is necessary where they work for the company to be successful. Report in class the next day.

- Have students and parents try the "All Aboard the Lifeboat" activity at home or with friends and see how many they can get "on board".

## [All Grade Levels]

# Cooperative Art

### Objective(s):

- To provide an opportunity for students to learn to cooperate on a single project
- Increase students' abilities to work cooperatively rather than competitively in the classroom.
- To help students learn to build on ideas of others and allow others to build on theirs

### Materials:

- Tables arranged such that six students can stand around the one large table(s) each with his/her own large sheet of art paper (2'X2')
- Paint brushes
- Various water color paints for each table
- Paper towels for each table
- Water dishes for each table
- One paint brush for each student
- Music on tape
- painting smocks for each student

### Lesson Plan:

*Introduction:* Ask students how many have ever played the children's game "musical chairs? Then tell them today we are going to experience the artist's version of that game. When the music begins, each student is to begin a drawing on the paper in front of them. When the music stops, each must immediately cease painting until the music resumes (no talking allowed during the game!)

*Activity:* Begin the music and let students start painting. After a minute or two, stop the music. Then instruct each student to move to the painting on their right, and begin adding to that painting when the music begins again. Continue this process until each group has gone around until everyone is back to their original painting.

*Closure:* Again follow the standard follow up questioning process. How did they feel when first had to move on to another painting? What did you do? How did you feel as you proceeded thru the activity? How did you feel when you saw your original painting at the end?

Have you ever experienced something similar to this (others adding to your ideas, projects, etc?). How did it go? How can we use what we've learned here for handling group projects more successfully?

## Suggested Classroom Follow-Up Activities:

- Have students engage in cooperative learning activities in class for math, science, social studies, etc.

- Have students take an exam on Monday for a lesson/skill/chapter they will be covering in the coming weeks and count the total number of correct responses for the class combined. Graph on a wall chart with vertical line = total correct answers in class and horizontal = day of the week. Retest each day with the class goal of trying to achieve a classroom PR (performance record) i.e. largest total number of correct responses to date . . . . the curve should eventually follow a J-curve profile.

## Suggested Home Follow-Up Activities:

- Have students engage in the same activity at home with their parents/family using paints or colored pencils. Title each picture and bring to class for sharing.

- Have students develop a creative story by each one writing one sentence and then moving to person next to them and adding a sentence to their story. Continue until everyone has added at least two sentences to each family member's story. Bring to class and share.

**[Elementary thru Middle School]**

# Community Planning

## Objective(s):

- To gain expertise in cooperative planning.
- To learn the importance of location, accessibility, and other variables in planning a large city.
- For students to gain expertise in the provision of help and encouragement to group mates.

## Materials:

- Assignment summary
- Key for symbols on a sheet
- Laminated, reusable landscape showing coastline, river, mountains, lake, forest, and island
- Overhead Projection pens
- One sheet of paper for justification
- Pen

## Lesson Plan:

*Introduction*: Randomly assign students to groups to ensure heterogeneity.

Assign Roles:

1. *Reader/Questioner*-To read all the materials and check for understanding within the group.
2. *Drawer*-To draw symbols on landscape.
3. Encourager/Observer-To recognize contributions and encourage good work from all group members; records the actions of each group member on an observation sheet while the group is working.
4. Recorder-To write down justification for placement of city facilities.
   Each member is randomly assigned a role.

*Activity:* Groups must design a city on a landscape board using various symbols to denote the apartments, factories, etc. They must justify the placements on a sheet of paper. The groups will then make a class demonstration of the landscape, with the other groups critically analyzing the placements.

## Instructional Task

- Reaching consensus is important to all placements. The teacher should make sure that all the students understand that they will be held accountable for understanding their justifications for their placements of the buildings, roads, etc. Explain that the teacher will randomly select two students out of the group to make the class presentation explaining placements and their justifications, so all must understand why and be able to explain the decisions of the group.

## Criteria for success:

- *Positive Interdependence:*
- Students must all agree on all placements of buildings and facilities. Each student is assigned a specific role in the group. Groups receive only one each of: landscape, key, explanation of assignment, limited color markers, and produce only one sheet of justifications for placements.
- *Individual Accountability:*
  Each member must be able to explain and justify to the class all placements on their landscape. They sign the justification sheet to signify their understanding and agreement with all placements.
- *Intergroup Cooperation*:
  * The groups compare their results when they are done. The groups have to identify at least two different placement strategies.
    Expected behaviors:
  * All group members explain step-by-step how they placed the roads, building, bridges, etc.
  * Group members ask for help when they do not understand how to solve a problem.
  * Group members encourage each other to participate by providing clear and accurate explanations and help.

*Closure:* Each group presents to the class their landscape design and the justification for the placements. Two students are randomly selected from each group to make the presentation. After each presentation all other groups are allowed two minutes to discuss and analyze the placements pros and cons. Each group must come up with three questions for the group that is presenting. For example, a group might ask why a dump was placed at the foot of the mountains far out of town when that would increase fuel costs and pollution from diesel exhaust. The presenting group is allowed 30 seconds to prepare the answer. Then a student from the presenting group makes the explanation and justification. Continue this procedure until all groups have presented.

*William G. Nicoll, PhD*

## Suggested Classroom Follow-Up Activities:

- Invite an architect or city planning board member to speak to your class regarding their job and how they try to take into account the needs of all people in designing the city or building.

- Have students work in small groups to build an bridge that will support a small toy car pulled by a string across it. must be at least two feet in length. Test the strength of each bridge by pulling the car across. Compare design ideas of each group.

## Suggested Home Follow-up Activities:

- Have parents and their child design their "ideal home" incorporating every family member's needs and special interests, etc. Share in class.

- Have parents conduct a family meeting to plan a "Family Day" over the weekend and come to a consensus among all members as to what they will do (**Note:** day must not carry price tag over $10). Have parents write about how they spent their 'family day' event.

# Cooperation Skills

## [Elementary Grades]

# Cooperative Machines

<u>Objective(s):</u>

- To experience the importance of working together
- To learn to solve problems via working together.

<u>Materials:</u>

- Board and Marker

<u>Lesson Plan:</u>

*Introduction:* Explain to the students that this unit will be on cooperation. Define cooperation; i.e., Cooperation is working together. Remind students that they will work with people in groups for the rest of their lives; brainstorm a list of ways they'll work in groups on the board.

*Activity:* Invite five or six students to who make Magnificent Machine in front of the class. Examples: a) A Chocolate Chip Cookie Machine – One person is a bowl, the second person pours the ingredients in, the third person stirs it up, the fourth person is the oven, the fifth person is a drying rack and the sixth person eats the cookie. B) Hand-Shaking Machine – One person puts a coin into the machine, the second person makes a noise like the coin rolling into the machine, the third person would make noise like the machine is moving something, the fourth person sticks their hand out shakes hands with person number one and the fifth person says 'Thank You!' in a robot voice.

Next, split the class into groups of five or six. Ask students to create their own machine. Have the students decide what kind of machine they want to make first. Give them about five to ten minutes to create their machine. Have each group come up to the front of the class to show their Magnificent Machine.

*Closure:* Ask each group to tell how well they cooperated and discuss what went well or didn't go well. Have the group rate how well they worked together on a scale of one to ten. Finish by reviewing the definition of cooperation and the importance of working together.

## Suggested Classroom Follow-Up Activities:

- Introduce the use of cooperative learning groups for class learning activities

- Assign students to small groups and give each a specific community, national or world problem (feeding homeless, children going hungry in Africa or U.S., litter, air/water pollution) and work together to design a plan for people to cooperate and solve this problem.


## Suggested Home Follow-Up Activities:

- Have parents identify with their child a problem to be solved in their home and then come up with a plan as to how they could better cooperate to solve the problem. Share ideas in class.

- Invite parents to develop their "family machine" at home . . . then have students share and recreate in class.

[Elementary Grades]

# Ant Families

## Objective(s):

- Students will learn about cooperation.
- Students will learn about ant communities.

## Materials:

- Ant Farm

## Lesson Plan:

*Introduction:* Open the lesson by talking about cooperation. When and why is cooperation necessary? Ask students if they think humans are the only ones who use cooperation to survive? Have students come up with other animals that cooperate in communities and write it on the board. Then talk about ant habitats and the different roles that each ant plays in order for their world to run smoothly.

*Activity:* Break the class into groups and have each group observe their own ant farm. Have the students discuss amongst one another what they are observing in the ant farm. Are all the ants working? Are any ants causing a disturbance or hurting each other? Then have them write a short story using the ants as their characters telling about a time when they had to work together for survival.

*Closure:* Conduct a class discussion about cooperation and ask students what would happen to the ant species if each individual ant only did what it wanted to do. How might this be applied to human beings?

## Suggested Classroom/Academic Follow-Up Activities:

- Have students write an essay or journal entry about the role of cooperation in their favorite "out of school" activity . . . e.g., sports teams, dance, music, etc

- Introduce a unit on bees and focus on cooperation among the bees. Invite a beekeeper in to speak to your students regarding bees, their behavior and making of honey.

- Introduce cooperative learning groups in your classroom. Have students work in teams on new math or science concepts and then give a quiz with the goal of all group members obtaining 80% or better. If a group fails, give more study/tutoring time until they can all re-take the quiz.

## Suggested Home Follow-Up Activities:

- Have parents make a list with their child of all the ways they cooperate as a family in their home.

- Have parents write a short description of how cooperation is important in their job.

[All Grade Levels]

# Group Tangle

**Objective(s):**

- Develop group cooperation skills
- Develop group problem solving skills
- Improve classroom cohesion

**Materials:**

None Needed

**Lesson Plan:**

*Introduction:* As students if they've ever found wires or rope in a tangled mess and tried to unravel the mess. Tell them that today we'll practice their skills in working together to untangle a mess of people.

*Activity:* Have the students stand in a circle facing toward the middle. Begin with groups of approximately ten students per group. Have the students hold hands. The teacher then enters each group as another member. The teacher then continues to hold the hand with one student on her left and releases the hand of the other student on her right. the teacher then tangles the group by winding them under and around one another (going under the hands of the students in the group) until finally arriving back to the other end of the chain and linking the hands of the two end students. the group must now, WITHOUT LETTING GO OF HANDS, get themselves back to their original circle.

*Closure:* Discuss how they managed to solve the problem and what they learned about effective group problem solving processes. Discuss how this skill can be used in the classroom and outside the classroom.

## Suggested Classroom Follow-Up Activities:

- Have students try the activity with larger groups, including the entire class. Invite them to share this activity with their school mates and/or friends and see how large a circle they can tangle and untangle.

- Have students engage in curriculum related problem solving activities such as building water rockets or labor saving inventions in science or making roller coasters from straws in math class.

- Have students take on an environmental or political current issue and develop a group solution to "untangle" that problem

## **Suggested Home Follow-Up Activities:**

- Have students share this activity with their family and/or friends and see how large a circle they can tangle and untangle.

- Have students interview their parents about a time when they had to work with people at their job to solve a problem; ask parents to write a short report for the class on examples of group problem solving in their workplace.

## [All Grade Levels]

# Paired Drawings

**Objective(s):**

- Develop students' cooperation skills
- Develop students ability to work in collaborative pairs
- Develop student's understanding and experience in non-verbal communication

**Materials:**

- Large sheets of plain drawing paper
- Colored pencils or paints (two colors per pair only)

**Lesson Plan:**

*Introduction:* Have students discuss times when they've had to work cooperatively with another person on a project, sport event, etc. How did it go? What worked? What caused problems?

*Activity:* Place students in pairs facing one another with a single sheet of drawing paper between them. Each student is given a crayon, colored pencil or paint brush. Each member of a pair should have a different color for the drawing but only one color per person. Inform students that this activity must be done in complete and total silence. No talking or gesturing is allowed!

Designate one person in each pairing to begin the drawing. When he/she completes a single line or brush stroke, he or she must then stop. Then the partner has a turn to make on line or brush stroke. this process continues back and forth until the teacher states the time is up —normally 5-10 minutes.

*Closure:* Have each group share their drawing with the class. Discuss with the class what they felt and observed happening between them as the activity proceeded. What was the end result?

## <u>Suggested Classroom Follow-Up Activities:</u>

- Assign class lessons requiring students to work in pairs (e.g., answering questions on science, social studies or math)

- Assign paired class science, math or social studies projects

## <u>Suggested Home Follow-Up Activities:</u>

- Have students complete a paired drawing with one or more family members and bring to class to discuss what evolved.

- Have parents and students brainstorm jobs and activities that require good communication and teamwork by paired individuals (e.g. beach volleyball, tennis doubles, trapeze artists, police officers, reporter and cameraman, etc). Combine into one list in class and post.

## Cooperation Skills

### [Elementary to Middle School]

# River Crossing

**Objective(s):**

- Develop students' team work skills
- Develop students' problem solving skills
- Develop a collaborative classroom climate

**Materials:**

- One foot square mats or cardboard squares for each student.
- Activity best done outdoors or in a gymnasium

**Lesson Plan:**

*Introduction:* Ask students how many have ever been on a sports team. Have them share why teamwork is important for a team sport. Then inform them that a classroom is much like a team sport. The goal is for the whole class to be successful by working together toward the same goal. Today, we are going to practice our teamwork skills.

*Activity:* Divide the class into teams of approximately 5 students each. Each member of a team is given a mat or square. Starting from behind one line, the team is told that their task is to cross to the other side ( a line placed about 15-20 yards away) without stepping in the piranha invested river (i.e. the floor or ground). They man only step on their mats. They must get the whole team across the river.

Give the students time to figure out a solution to this problem. (solution is normally to lay down one mat at a time until there is a student on each mat heading across the river, then the last student shares space on the mat with the student in front of him and passes the vacated, last mat, up the line to be placed in front . . . all members then proceed one step and continue the process until all are across . . . other solutions may also be found)

*Closure:* Go thru the Concluding Questions process for these classroom guidance lessons. End By asking the students to brainstorm ways to improve our classroom's teamwork to make sure everyone is successful this year.

## Suggested Classroom Follow-Up Activities:

- Introduce cooperative learning activities for completing class assignments; e.g. teams must pass the mastery test in a math skill by having each student able to complete the test with 90% or better correct, teams study together/tutor one another and re-take the test until all five members pass.

- Have students work in teams for science or social studies projects. Have the teams work out each "player's" task and then combine into a single project presentation in class.

- End class each day by having students share an example of how a classmate was a good "teammate" today. Students must identify a specific act of teamwork in the classroom.


## Suggested Home Follow-Up Activities:

- Have parents complete a brief description of how teamwork is important in their place of work. Read in class or make a class "book" with everyone's homework included.

- Have parents watch a team sporting event together and list examples of "cooperation" and teamwork by the players. Share the lists in class.

- Have parents work with their child to develop a list of "Ways we work as a team at home".

# Responsible Contribution Skills

# Options for Alternative Actions

## Objective(s):

- To help students find viable solutions to problematic social situations
- To help students understand they always have options for their responses
- To help students consider likely consequences when choosing their responses.

## Materials:

- Options Worksheet
- Prepared scenarios in school, home, in the community or with peers that are typical to the life situations of your students.

## Lesson Plan:

*Introduction:* Share with the students a true story from your life about a decision you once made that you'd like to do over again, but handle differently. Ask the students to share events from their own lives about which they now wish they had chosen to handle differently. Inform students that today we are going to be learning a process for making good decisions in our lives.

*Activity:* Place students in small work groups of three to four students each. Give each group an "Options Worksheet". Inform students that for each scenario you read, they will, as a group, complete the six questions on the worksheet and then share their answers with the class. Read activity #1. Have students complete their answers as a group and then share responses with the entire class. Continue with at least two more scenarios.

*Closure:* Follow the Developing Resilient Youth's Concluding Discussion format.

## Suggested Classroom Follow-Up Activities:

- During reading/literature class, stop occasionally and utilize the Options Worksheet process to discuss what the characters are most likely to do, options they have, possible consequences of each, etc. Then proceed to read what option the character chose.

- Assign a writing activity in which students write on the topic of, "If I could do it over again". Students choose an event in their lives that they would like to go back and re-do so it turns out better.

- Repeat the Options for Alternative Actions activity during the week with other scenarios which are typical in the daily lives of your students.

## Suggested Home Follow-Up Activities:

- Have parents write an "If I could do it over again" story from their own lives and share with their son/daughter.

- Have parents read a story to their son/daughter and then together make up a list of options the main character had during the story as to how he/she might act or respond to the various situations and have them identify likely outcomes of those alternative actions.

- Have parents share a story with their child about a time they made a decision to handle an event in their lives that was difficult but for which they are today quite proud. Share these in class.

# Options for Alternative Actions
## Worksheet

| **Options** | **Event #1** | **Event #2** | **Event #3** |
| --- | --- | --- | --- |

What are you most likely to do?

What else could you do? (minimum of two)?

What would the likely consequences be of
each option?

What option would have the worst consequences?

What would probably have the most favorable,
long range consequences? for you? for others?

What would you feel most proud about doing? why?

What might you decide to do the next time you are
in such a situation.

## [Middle to High School]

# <u>Lean on Me</u>

<u>Objective(s):</u>

- Develop students empathy skills
- Foster a caring and supportive classroom climate
- Increase awareness of times when we face choices to help or hurt others
- Increase awareness that "I'm not involved" is never an option in life.

<u>Materials:</u>

- Choose any book dealing with a true life situation where an individual needed the help of others to survive.

<u>Lesson Plan:</u>

*Introduction:* Begin by playing the song, Lean on Me. Ask students to discuss a time when they needed someone (friend, parent, etc) to lean on in order to get through a difficult time. Inform students that the class will be reading books describing such situations over the next couple weeks.

*Activity:* Discuss the role of a bully, a victim and the bystanders in any type of conflict or injustice situation. Then read to the class a chapter each day from one of the books listed below with the focus on identifying who are the bullies, the victims and the bystanders.

*Closure:* Following each chapter, discuss with the class how they think each character felt and why they may have decided to act as they did in that situation.

## <u>Suggested Books:</u>

1. <u>Diary of Anne Frank</u> (Frank, A, Diary of girl in early teens kept in hiding from Nazi occupation in the Netherlands.

2. <u>Your Name is Renee</u> (Cretzmeyer, S., 1999) Story of Ruth Kapp Hartz's experience as a hidden child in Nazi occupied France. Oxford University Press.

3. <u>A Long Way Gone</u> (Beah, Ishmael, 2007. Memoirs of a 12 year old boy forced to become a boy soldier in Sierra Leone, Africa and his eventual rehabilitation.

4. <u>I am Nujood, age 10 and divorced</u>. (2008). Nujood Ali & Delphine Minoui. Story of young Yemen girl's sale into marriage and fight for her freedom.

## Suggested Classroom Follow-Up Activities:

- Have small groups of students choose a similar book from a list prepared by your librarian to read, discuss and write their reaction to as a class assignment.

- Invite in a guest speaker who has been in a situation of helping or being helped during a stressful time (hurricane, tsunami, war, genocide, holocaust, homelessness, catastrophic events, etc). Have them tell their story and then open class up for question/answers.

- Invite students to write essays regarding "A time when I let a friend "lean on me".

- Have the students learn the song, *"Lean on Me"* in music

- Have the students research various individuals who were responsible (altruistic) bystanders in history, individuals who displayed "heroic altruism" in situations dangerous to themselves (Examples: Miep Gies, Varian Fry, Albert Goering, Emile Schindler, Kurt Gerstein, Wilm Hosenfeld, Berthold Beitz, Nelson Mandela, Mahatma Ghandi, Martin Luther King, John Adams, Emile Schindler, Hans Hedtoft, Georg Duckwitz, Harriet Tubman, Paul Rosesabaagina, Pinchas Tibor Rosenbaum, etc.)

- Have students write in their journals how they view Dante's quote as it applies to us as Bystanders in regard to issues such as bullying, domestic violence, child abuse, poverty, homelessness, child labor, sex/slave trade, and other adverse life conditions impacting the lives of people today, *"The hottest places in hell are reserved for those who in time of great moral crises maintain their neutrality."*

## Suggested Home Follow-Up Activities:

- Ask students to interview a parent or family member about a time they stepped in and let someone lean on them when times were bad.

- Have students identify a local group (village, homeless, children's home, etc) who need a lending hand to help them survive and develop a home-school partnership to assist.

- Arrange an opportunity for parents and students to participate in a volunteer activity to enrich the lives of those in need . . . (for ideas see book, by Friedman, J. & Roehlkepartain, J. (2010) "Doing Good Together". Minneapolis, MN: Free Spirit Press.)

## Responsible Contribution Skills

### [All Grade Levels]

# Choices We All Have

<u>Objective(s):</u>

- Help students become aware of how much control/responsibility they have over their own lives.
- Help students accept responsibility for their actions in situations where they have control

<u>Materials:</u>

- Prepared "Choices" worksheet with 4 columns. List various daily activities down the left column with other three columns marked at the top: Myself, My Teachers, My Parents

<u>Lesson Plan:</u>

*Introduction:* Ask how many students have ever felt like people were always trying to tell them what to do, how to act and controlling their lives. Explain that sometimes we forget to recognize how independent we all are and how much control we have over our own lives. But with this "control" comes recognition that we are responsible for what we do or don't do.

*Activity:* Hand out the "Choices" worksheet and ask students to put an X in the column for each item indicating whether they think they or someone else decides each of these things in their life. Read the list to the students so the class does it all together. Remind students to no say anything until all done so we can compare our ideas, thoughts on each item.Upon completing the Choices list, have the students stand. Review each question and have students move to one of three pre-designated spots indicating if their answer to that question was: myself, my teacher or my parents. Invite a brief discussion from each group as to why they chose that answer. have students return to their desks (standing) and repeat the process for the additional questions.

*Closure:* Ask the students if they've ever said, "he/she made me do it" or "he/she made me angry, sad", etc. Based on today's discussion, who can think of anything someone else can "make us do" or feel if we don't want to? Have students comment on what Eleanor Roosevelt meant when she said, "Nobody can hurt my feelings without my permission".

## Suggested Classroom Follow-Up Activities:

- Have students identify something they would choose to learn more about if in charge of the school curriculum. Then have them develop a plan for learning more about that topic during a free learning time period in class or out of class. Ask students to report back on what they learned.

- During reading and social studies class lessons, discuss the choices various individuals or characters made in their life. What options did each have? Why do you suppose he/she chose to act and feel as he/she did?

- Begin each day with students identifying one thing they have chosen to learn, accomplish, or improve in today. Then close the school day by having students report on how successful they were in achieving their goal and what they did to make it successful or to sabotage their own goals.

## Suggested Home Follow-Up Activities:

- Ask parents to complete a short paragraph regarding a choice they made in their life for which they are very proud today along with a choice they now regret having made and how they would handle that situation if they had a second chance. Read the essays in class.

- Have parents and students make a list of the things at home which the student chooses to do or not do in his /her life.

- Have parents write a short paragraph on, "A time my son/daughter made a choice that made me proud to be his/her parent".

# SAMPLE WORKSHEET

## *Choices We All Have*

| Action | Myself | Teachers | Parents |
|---|---|---|---|
| What I eat | | | |
| When I sleep | | | |
| When I go to bed | | | |
| How I spend my money | | | |
| When I get up | | | |
| When I study | | | |
| When I make a friend | | | |
| When I clean my room | | | |
| When I daydream | | | |
| What I think | | | |
| How I feel | | | |
| What I wear to school | | | |
| What I read | | | |
| What I enjoy doing | | | |
| When I smile | | | |
| When I feel angry | | | |
| When I feel sad | | | |
| What I do during school time | | | |
| What we'll study today | | | |
| What time we'll have lunch | | | |
| What I'll eat for lunch | | | |
| What I'll have to eat for lunch | | | |
| What I'll learn today | | | |

## Responsible Contribution Skills
### Grades: K-8

# Using Literature to Teach About Bullying

**Objective(s):**

- Students will recognize the signs of bullying
- Students will be able to employ strategies to prevent bullying situations

**Materials:**

- The Bully by Judith Casely
- Lily's Secret by Imou Miko
- Hooway for Wodney Wat by Helen Lester
- Crickwing by Janell Cannon

**Lesson Plan:**

*Introduction:* Read aloud the four stories listed in the Materials section above. After reading each story, discuss the following questions.

- Who is the bully?
- Why is this character acting like a bully?
- What types of bullying do you see in this story?
- How might the character being bullied handle the bully?

[Alternative strategy: Arrange students into small groups. Ask each group to read one of the books on the list and respond to the questions.]

*Activity:* Discuss/brainstorm the following vocabulary words as a class or in smaller student groups. Create an acceptable definition for each word.

- bullying
- conflict
- resolution
- violence
- gossip
- exclusion

Have students work in small cooperative groups; give each group one of the types of bullying listed below. Have each group discuss examples of that type of bullying. Group members should be prepared to discuss the harm that can result from that kind of bullying and to offer more positive ways to treat others as well as what one can do when he/she observes someone being bullied in this way.

- gossip
- exclusion
- physical bullying
- verbal bullying

***Closure:*** After students share their problems and solutions, bring the class back together and have students create a contract for acceptable behavior in their classroom.

## Suggested Classroom/Academic Follow-Up Activities:

- Have students explain how they might apply what they've learned to situations outside the classroom.

- Have students create posters displaying positive behavior.

- Have the class brainstorm and research historical events that were the result of bullying on a global scale (e.g., the Holocaust).

## Suggested Home Follow-Up Activities:

- Have students interview a parent or family member regarding a time they witnessed someone being bullied or mistreated and what they did to stop the mistreatment.

- Have students brainstorm with family members what one can do to stop bullying and abusive behaviors when we are a) the victim or b) the bystander.

- Provide parents with a list of books and/or movies in which bullying occurs. Ask them to read or watch one of these with their child this week and write a brief report on what they learned and discussed from this book/video.

# Open Ended Stories

### Objective(s):

- To develop problem solving skills related to typical social situations
- To increase students' awareness of behavioral alternatives or options in various situations
- To increase abilities to empathize and use this skill for more effective and responsible behavior choices.

### Materials:

- Series of teacher developed open-ended stories to be read to the class dealing with typical social interaction issues including bullying, school failure, making friends, and so forth.

### Lesson Plan:

*Introduction:* Inform students that today we are going to work on our creative thinking and problem solving skills in social situations. Ask for examples of difficult situations they have encountered with other people and how they chose to solve the problem.

*Activity:* Divide the class into working groups of 3-4 students per group. Provide each group with a copy of three Open-Ended Stories. Read the stories as a class and then have each group write an ending to the story describing how each person felt, what motivated their actions and how someone might act to help this story end in a positive, constructive manner.

*Closure:* Follow the Developing Resilient Youth's Concluding Discussion format.

## Suggested Classroom Follow-Up Activities:

- Repeat the activity several times during the week with differing Open-Ended stories.

- Have students complete a writing assignment in which they develop a common problematic social situation in school or at home for which they then write a creative and positive solution.

- In history class, provide students with a description of dilemmas faced by various historical figures. Ask them to come up with how they would handle the situation and their rationale for this solution. Then read and discuss the "rest of the story" as that historical figure actually chose to respond. Have students discuss the consequences (pro and con) of the decision and what might have occurred if their decision was followed instead.

## <u>Suggested Home Follow-Up Activities:</u>

- Give students an Open Ended story to bring home and have their parents complete so as to compare with what the students did in school.

- Ask parents to send in a description of a "problematic situation" they recently encountered at work. Invite students to come up with solutions to the situation.

- Ask parents to compose their own "open ended story" based on difficult situations children might encounter in the school, home, or community. Use these for class writing assignments or discussion topics.

## [All Grade Levels]

# Worriers versus Solvers Game

<u>**Objective(s):**</u>

- Assist students in identifying common worries, fears and concerns shared among all students
- Assist students in identifying options they have for solving such worries, fears and concerns.
- Develop students' problem solving skills

<u>**Materials:**</u>

- List of common problems, worries, fears and concerns of children in this age group.
- Blackboard or newsprint with markers

<u>**Lesson Plan:**</u>

*Introduction:* Ask students how many have ever felt worried, stressed or fearful when having to face a new situation or experience in their life. Invite students to share some of the situations in which they've experienced these feelings. After some initial sharing, tell the students that today we are going to stage our own "Game Show" to see how good we are at both Worrying and Solving problems such stressful situations in life.

*Activity:* Divide the class into teams of 5 students each. Invite two of the teams to come to the front of the room and sit behind their respective 6foot tables placed on either side of the room. Designate one team, "The Worriers" and the other team, "The Solvers".

- The task of the Worrier team is to suggest things that might go wrong, or be scary for each situation identified by the teacher (aka: game show host).
- The task of the Solver team is to suggest solutions to the problem posed by the Worrier team members. If the problem is one that has no solution over which the student has control, then answers should focus on how one could make the best of such a bad situation.
- Team points will be marked on the board or newsprint. One point for each "worry" and one point for each "solution". Teams have ten seconds to answer (have a time keeper and a buzzer or bell to indicate time limit passed). If a team cannot come up with an answer within the time limit, the other team gets the point.

- Begin the game by stating one common situation in student's lives that could cause them to worry or be fearful, stressed, etc. (e.g., "first day at a new school"). Team collaboration is encouraged (similar to "Family Feud" on U.S. television)
- The first Worrier team member identifies something one might fear could go wrong. The first Solver team member then must identify a possible solution. Again, team collaboration in arriving at an answer is encouraged.
- After playing a round, switch teams until everyone has had the chance to play as both the Worriers and the Solvers.

*Possible Topics:* First day at new school; Having to read aloud or speak in front of the class; Moving to a new neighborhood, country, state; Choosing your wardrobe for the new school year; Taking an exam in class; Going someplace without your parents (school trip, camp, etc); Being confronted by a bully in school; Trying out for a new team, club or activity (soccer team, band, drama, etc); Asking someone to go out with you, to a dance, etc . . . include situations specific to your students and grade level.

*Closure:* Have the students briefly discussed which they found easier to do, worrying or solving problems? Introduce the concept of the 3 F's in responding to fear: Fight, Flight or Freeze. Discuss what experiences they have had in responding with one of these three fear response behaviors.

## Suggested Classroom Follow-Up Activities:

- For science, have students research different animals and their typical response to fear, i.e. fight, flight or freeze and how/why this works for them (i.e. natural adaptation).

- Invite in a classroom speaker who has faced extremely dangerous situations (e.g. soldier in combat, firefighter, SWAT policeman, pilot, etc). Have them discuss the fears and how they dealt with it in their lives.

- Have students in "book club" groups (or read to the class) read biographies or autobiographies of historical figures and identify what fears they each faced and how they dealt with it. (e.g. Martin Luther King, King Henry V, John Adams, George Washington, Sitting Bull, Nelson Mandela, Mahatma Ghandi, etc).

## Suggested Home Follow-Up Activities:

- Have students interview their parents regarding "A time in my (parent's) life when I felt very fearful or worried". Ask parents to discuss how they handled it (including a time they handled it well versus a time I didn't handle it so well (include how they would handle that situation better now). Share these in class.

- Have parents and students complete a list of things we all need to worry about today and what we can all do to solve the problem. (e.g. environment, war, poverty, etc.) Share in class.

- Have parents complete a "Things I worry about in raising my son/daughter". Down one column parents list the fears etc they experience as a parent. In the second column they identify what they do to try to solve these concerns and fears.

<u>**Example**</u>:

| <u>**Worry About:**</u> | <u>**Do About my Worries:**</u> |
|---|---|
| That he/she will get hurt | teach safety skills, supervise activities |
| That he/she won't be successful | Encourage studying. |
| That he/she will use drugs | talk about drugs, warn, etc. |

## [All Grade Levels]

# Random Acts of Kindness

### Objective(s):

- Make students more aware of their responsibility to help others
- Help students understand that to ignore a wrong is to condone its continuance
- Improve student awareness of what they can do to help others

### Materials:

- Kyle story (attached)
- Newsprint for brainstorming in small groups
- Bulletin Board marked "Random Acts of Kindness"

### Lesson Plan:

*Introduction:* Begin by reading the story of "Kyle". Discuss with the class the consequences of stopping to help versus passing a distressed person without stopping to help. What do you communicate to that person? To the "bullies" who knocked his books out? How do you feel toward the bullies, passers-by and those who stop to help?

*Activity:* Have students meet in small groups of 3-4 persons to brainstorm lists of things they can do as "Random Acts of Kindness" in their school and community. Compare and combine their lists and post in the classroom.

*Closure:* Discuss how one feels when they observe, receive and commit a random act of kindness. Challenge students to make a commitment to engage in at least one random act of kindness daily for the week. Start each day with students reporting what they did and how it was received.

### Suggested Classroom Follow-Up Activities:

- Acknowledge observed random acts of kindness on a class bulletin board daily.

- Invite other teachers, staff and administrators to hand out "Random Acts of Kindness" recognition slips to students "caught" doing so.

- Assign class readings or projects regarding "random acts of kindness" which take place in our world daily (e.g. peace corps volunteers, AmeriCorps, Hurricane Katrina, SE Asian Tsunami and other catastrophes and how some responded, soup kitchens, UN rescue of Child Soldiers in Africa, etc).

- Invite the class to pick a "class random act" for the school or community and follow thru.

## **Suggested Home Follow-Up Activities:**

- Have students perform "random acts of kindness" at home and report on what they did.

- Ask parents to write a short story of a time they "stopped to help" someone in distress.

- Ask parents to write a short story about a time someone stopped to help them and how they felt about it.

## Responsible Contribution Skills

[Grades 3-12]

# Mentoring Buddies

<u>**Objective(s):**</u>

- Develop a caring community of learners
- Develop student's skills in caring for and assisting younger students
- Develop student's sense of responsible contribution to their school community

<u>**Materials:**</u>

- Large sheets of brown paper
- Drawing or painting supplies

<u>**Lesson Plan:**</u>

*Introduction:* Discuss with the class what the terms "role model" and "mentor" means to them. Ask the students to share who those individuals are that they consider to be role models in their lives and why. Then, inform the students that this year the class will "adopt" a class of younger students. It will be our goal to serve as both role models and tutor/mentors to help those young students grow both academically and as responsible, caring individuals.

*Activity:* Have the two classes (older mentors and young pre-school to primary aged) meet in an auditorium, gym or cafeteria setting. Have the younger students draw the names of their "mentor buddies" out of a hat. As they draw the name, each mentor steps forward and finds a spot to sit with their new buddy. Provide each student with a large sheet (4-6') sheet of brown paper and drawing supplies. Instruct the older students draw life-sized outlines of their new young buddy on the paper. Then have the younger students do the same thing with their mentor buddy. Give them some time to color in their life-sized self portraits. Be sure names of each student are placed in large letters on their drawings (e.g. chest, pant leg).

*Closure:* If possible, find some wall space for the students to hang their drawings on the wall of the younger grades classroom. Inform students that each week they will meet for about 20-30 minutes with their "buddy". During those times the older students will serve as tutors (reading to them, assisting with projects or helping tutor them with any school work they may find challenging) Schedule times for the coming week.

## Suggested Classroom Follow-Up Activities:

- Schedule time at least twice weekly for the older students to meet with and serve as mentors/tutors for their "little buddy". The teacher may want to suggest academic skills to work on or interests of the younger student for the tutor to read about with them. Each week take out the life-sized drawings and have the students write next to their "self-portrait" something they learned that week from their Mentoring Buddy. The older mentoring buddy can do the same for things he/she has learned working with their little buddy that week.

- Have the Mentor Buddies maintain a journal in which they write about what they are learning and experiencing from being a mentor and to outline their plans for the next mentor/tutoring session. The teacher can review these journals periodically both to assess writing skills and to provide suggestions and feedback regarding their tutoring "lesson plans".

- Assign students a history lesson in which they must identify the great "mentors" of history and discuss how they helped others, or someone in particular, to achieve or succeed in life.

## Suggested Home Follow-Up Activities:

- Ask parents to write about someone who served as a mentor in their lives and how that person has impacted their life. Share the stories in class.

- Ask students to interview a grandparent, uncle or neighbor about people who have been mentors to them or helped them succeed and grow in some way.

- Have parents complete a "My Life Mentors" worksheet answering questions such as: Who taught you to read? Who taught you to ride a bike? Play baseball, soccer, or some favorite sport? To do your job? To be a parent? etc., etc. Have parents share their stories about these people with their child.

- Have students and their parents work together to make a list of "Characteristics of Great Mentors". Instruct them to think of the best teacher or mentors they have had in their lives and what those people did special that made them so effective in contributing to your life.

# Independent Learning Groups

### Objective(s):

- Assist students in taking responsibility for their own learning/education
- Increase parent involvement in the curriculum
- Increase learning motivation in students

### Materials:

- None needed

### Lesson Plan:

*Introduction:* Ask the students to imagine that they are going to be able to open their own school and decide what to include in the curriculum. Think about what things you'd most like to learn about.

*Activity:* Brainstorm a list and put on newsprint to hang on the classroom wall. Then have students look over the lists and find four other people who are interested in the same topic. Students then are to sit with their group and develop ideas for what they'd like to learn on that topic and how they might go about learning more. The teacher can then send the list to parents requesting volunteers to teach a group of five or more students a lesson or two on their chosen topic.

*Closure:* Schedule time over the next week or two for each group to research their topic and have a lesson from a parent or local "volunteer" expert on the subject. Students can also be asked to teach the class a little about their topic also once their lessons/research is completed.

### Suggested Classroom Follow-Up Activities:

- Schedule time during the week for the student groups to be involved in researching and learning about their topic.

- Schedule additional times for Independent Learning Groups. Include a sign-up sheet such that whenever five or more students sign up with an interest in any one topic, the teacher can seek parents or other volunteers to provide instruction.

- When introducing a new chapter or topic in history or science, begin by asking students to identify what they'd like to learn on this subject prior to starting instruction. Try to be sure to cover this information in the lesson plans or have students independently pursue that information and report to the class as a whole.

## Suggested Home Follow-Up Activities:

- Send the list of chosen topics home to the parents and request volunteers to teach one of the desired topics to a small group of students.

- Have parents discuss with their child what things they've always wanted to learn more about. Then develop a "family plan" to all learn about that subject. Send in the family lesson plan to share with the class. Later ask for a "family learning project report" when they are done.

- If several parents identify a similar topic, seek ways to have an evening or weekend family learning night on that topic.

[Elementary Grades]

# Being Prepared

## Objective:

To assist students in recognizing the importance of being prepared for the tasks they are expected to perform.

## Materials:

Small carry-all bag with a few sporting items inside (use items from one sport, purposely omit some needed items and include a couple items from another sport as well).

## Lesson:

### Introduction:

Explain to the class that you are going to play in a soccer game after school and that you'd like the class to go through the items in your bag with you to make sure that you didn't forget anything. Use one volunteer to help you (dress the student in your sporting equipment as you go). Hold up each item as you pull it out of the bag and place it on the student. After the student is fully dressed with the items from your bag, begin a discussion about your equipment.

I.E.,    "What's wrong with my soccer bag?"

"What else do you think I'll need in order to be able to play?"

"Am I prepared for my game this afternoon?"

"Looks like I am not being very responsible since I didn't come with the items I'll need for the game. How will this affect my teammates?"

"What do I need to be a responsible member of the team?"

"How will my being irresponsible and not planning ahead effect the other 10 players on my team?"

"Why do we need to be responsible?"

### Activity

*Step 1:* Let's brainstorm about some times in our lives when we each need to be responsible to ourselves and to others (make a list on the chalkboard, newsprint or overhead).

*Step 2:* Are there specific times in school when we need to be responsible? Start a new chart or overhead with the heading: **School Responsibilities**. Write down as many suggestions as the students offer or as time allows.

*Step 3:* Discuss why it is important to be responsible in school. Have the students tell what happens when we don't fulfill each of these responsibilities and how that affects others in the class as well as ourselves.

***Closure:***

Discuss: A What did you think when I came in and my bag was missing equipment and had wrong equipment for the game today?@

"What did you learn from today's lesson?"

"What is one thing that you can do this week to be a more responsible person?" (Go around the classroom and give each student a chance to identify a target behavior). Be sure to comment to each student during the week when you see them meeting their responsibility goal.

## Suggested Classroom Follow-Up Activities:

- Working in small groups, have the students create stories (they can write them or dictate to the teacher, parent volunteer or an aide) around the theme of being responsible: e.g., Surviving Ms. Irresponsible's Classroom: begin by offering an opening sentence such as; "Once there was a first grade teacher named Ms Irresponsible. Every day she acted irresponsibly and forgot to come to class prepared. They had to find ways to learn and make their classroom successful in spite of her behavior. For example, one day . . . . .". Students can share their group stories or have them combined into an anthology of readings on Ms. Irresponsible.

- Change the **"I SPY" Bulletin Board** to focus on "I Spied These Responsible Students"; each day add new examples of students in your class displaying responsible behaviors observed in class and around the school.

- Link to a Social Studies lesson on Community Workers and what responsibilities each must remember to do each day so as to do his/her job for our community.

## Suggested Home Follow-Up Activities:

- Have students interview their parents regarding responsibilities they have at their work and what they must remember to do, prepare or bring each day to do their job as well as what would happen if they acted irresponsibly and forgot. Have them share the answers in class.

- Have students complete a homework worksheet titled, "***How Our Family Works***"@. With parental assistance, the students complete the list of household tasks/responsibilities of each family member at home (mother, fathers, brothers and sisters).

- Compile a list of responsibilities your students have at home and make a bulletin board listing "What _____ Graders Can Do to Help at Home". Then send a copy of the list home to all parents.

- Ask parents to write a short description of a time when their son/daughter's responsible behavior at home helped them or the family. Have students read these in class the next day.

For further information on the *Developing Resilient Youth program*, additional materials or to obtain information on training program for your school staff, agency or organization

**Contact:**
*William G. Nicoll, Ph.D.,*
**The Resilience Counseling & Training Center,**
**1555 St Lucie West Blvd,**
**Port St Lucie, Florida 34986;**
**Email: resiliencectc@aol.com**
**www.resiliencecounselingcenter.com**